# The Presence In The Promise

*First Lesson Sermons For Advent/Christmas/Epiphany Cycle C*

## Harry N. Huxhold

CSS Publishing Company, Inc., Lima, Ohio

THE PRESENCE IN THE PROMISE

Copyright © 2000 by
CSS Publishing Company, Inc.
Lima, Ohio

All rights reserved. No part of this publication may be reproduced in any manner whatsoever without the prior permission of the publisher, except in the case of brief quotations embodied in critical articles and reviews. Inquiries should be addressed to: Permissions, CSS Publishing Company, Inc., P.O. Box 4503, Lima, Ohio 45802-4503.

**Library of Congress Cataloging-in-Publication Data**

Huxhold, Harry N.
    The presence in the promise : first lesson sermons for Advent/Christmas/Epiphany, cycle C / Harry N. Huxhold.
    p. cm.
    ISBN 0-7880-1713-6 (alk. paper)
    1. Advent sermons. 2. Christmas sermons. 3. Epiphany season—Sermons. 4. Bible. O.T.— Sermons. 5. Srmons, American. 6. Lectionary preaching. I. Title.
BV4254.5 .H89 2000
252'.61—dc20                                                       00-35793
                                                                                      CIP

This book is available in the following formats, listed by ISBN:
    0-7880-1713-6    Book
    0-7880-1714-4    Disk
    0-7880-1715-2    Sermon Prep

For more information about CSS Publishing Company resources, visit our website at www.csspub.com.

PRINTED IN U.S.A.

*To
The Members
of
King of Glory Lutheran Church
Carmel, Indiana
with
Appreciation and Affection
in
Christ*

# Table Of Contents

| | |
|---|---|
| **Introduction** | 7 |
| **Advent 1** <br> Days Of Promise <br> Jeremiah 33:14-16 | 9 |
| **Advent 2** <br> A Messenger Of Promise <br> Malachi 3:1-4 | 17 |
| **Advent 3** <br> A Song Of Promise <br> Zephaniah 3:14-20 | 25 |
| **Advent 4** <br> A Town Of Promise <br> Micah 5:2-5a | 33 |
| **Christmas Eve/Day** <br> The Child Of Promise <br> Isaiah 9:2-7 | 39 |
| **Christmas 1** <br> The Promising Child <br> 1 Samuel 2:18-20, 26 | 47 |
| **Christmas 2** <br> The Children Of Promise <br> Jeremiah 31:7-14 | 53 |
| **Epiphany** <br> The Promise Of Sight <br> Isaiah 60:1-6 | 61 |

**Epiphany 1**     69
**(Baptism Of Our Lord)**
  The Promise Of Baptism
  Isaiah 43:1-7

**Epiphany 2**     77
  Light For Beauty
  Isaiah 62:1-5

**Epiphany 3**     85
  Light From The Word
  Nehemiah 8:1-3, 5-6, 8-10

**Epiphany 4**     93
  The Light Touch
  Jeremiah 1:4-10

**Epiphany 5**     101
  Light To Serve
  Isaiah 6:1-8 (9-13)

**Epiphany 6**     109
  The Fruit Of One's Doings
  Jeremiah 17:5-10

**Epiphany 7**     117
  The Fruit Of Forgiveness
  Genesis 45:3-11, 15

**Epiphany 8**     125
  The Fruit Of The Word
  Isaiah 55:10-13

**The Transfiguration Of Our Lord**     133
**(Last Sunday After The Epiphany)**
  Keeping The Glow On
  Exodus 34:29-35

# Introduction

The Post-Communion canticle in one of the settings of the Lutheran Liturgy sings out, "He recalls his promises and leads his people forth in joy with shouts of thanksgiving. Alleluia." This concluding song of the celebration of word and sacrament reminds us that the worship of the Christian congregation holds out rich promise for the worshipers. The joyful phrase, "He recalls his promises," also alerts the worshipers to recognize the lively application of word and sacrament they have just experienced is as fresh as the promises of hope, providence, salvation, grace, and steadfast love God first shared with humanity millennia ago.

The First Lessons appointed for the liturgical Sundays and festivals of the Church Year inform the worshipers that what God has revealed in the life, death, and resurrection of our Lord Jesus Christ, God had also revealed in the history of God's ancient people Israel. Through faithful prophets and various means God revealed to the people of God in ancient Israel what God had done, was doing, and would be doing for them in divine providential care and redeeming love. God also revealed the fullness of the divine love in the promise of a messianic figure. However, in the process of offering the promise of the messianic age, God already wrapped the ancient hearers in the same grace and love by which the Messiah came. The reading and hearing of the First Lessons appointed from the Hebrew Scriptures are well matched to the Holy Gospels appointed for the same day. The First Lesson and the Gospel are mutually informative of what God continues to do in grace for people who gladly hear what God would speak to them.

Interpreters of Scriptures can say that we cannot understand the New Testament of the Bible unless we understand the Old Testament. It is unfortunate we use the term "Old" Testament, because the Hebrew Scriptures are always as fresh as the "New." Luther would say that in order to understand the New Testament, first we have to become good Jews, that is, to think Hebraically. He would also say that if we want to know how God will treat the Christian Church, we have to look how God treated the ancient people Israel.

The following sermons are based on the First Readings of The Revised Common Lectionary for the seasons Advent through Epiphany. These lessons are especially helpful in demonstrating the possibilities of illustrating how dependent we are upon the revelations God gave to the ancient people Israel and how God "recalls his promises."

The title of my first book of sermons on the Old Testament was *The Promise And The Presence*. This volume tightens that up a bit with *The Presence In The Promise*. May the preacher find joy in adding to and improving upon what is found here.

Harry N. Huxhold

*Advent 1*

# Days Of Promise

*Jeremiah 33:14-16*

---

**Without a doubt** the most troubling time in the history of the United Sates was the Civil War era. Devastated by the ruins of war, the country was drained emotionally and spiritually. The hostility had developed not only between regions of the country, but it spilled over into families and institutions. At given moments of the war, people questioned whether they would ever be able to recover from the debacle that had been wrought upon the nation. The future was in grave doubt. People lost their perspective on all time, because the period was so traumatic. They found it impossible to imagine the future or any type of recovery. After Gettysburg, General Meade wrote that he had lived thirty years in the last ten days. The young Henry Adams, on a mission in London with his father, wrote that people lived these momentous days "without a second thought, what at another time would be the event of a year, perhaps a life." The people lived in such turmoil in their depressed state they thought they could never get their lives together again.

In the First Lesson appointed for today we hear a prophetic word written at a time when the people of God would have to face similar circumstances. The people would be immobilized by the prospects of a lack of defense against the siege of their city by the Babylonians and their ultimate defeat which had been predicted in a prophetic word from the Prophet Jeremiah. However, even as the prophetic word could be realistic about the tragic fate that would engulf the people, the prophetic word could also hold out the hope of days of promise. The prophet could proclaim a word about days of promise, because God always can and does offer a word of deliverance and hope for us.

**The Days Are Coming**

For Jeremiah the word of hope begins, "The days are surely coming, says the Lord." The future is in the hands of God. That is the premise for what the prophet has to reveal. All of history, according to the prophet, is in the hands of God. The prophet was convinced that God is the mover and shaker of history. Regardless of how large the events are, or how far-reaching the affairs of the rulers of the earth are, God is the One who ultimately decides how things will turn out for the benefit of God's people.

Obviously, the rulers of this world, and the people of any age are not always cognizant of God's will or purposes. People tend to frustrate the will of God. They can be hostile to the will of God. God must work around and against the will of those who oppose God. That can mean God must also work through the people opposed to the divine will. The result is that God must set the stage for working out God's purposes through whatever is at hand. God chooses the right time, the propitious hour, and the most helpful circumstances for achieving the divine goals. In Advent, as we prepare for the observance of the Birth of our Lord, we think of how God chose the most favorable moment for the birth of our Lord and the most advantageous time for the expansion of Christianity. The Apostle Paul could speak of that as the "fullness of time."

**Fulfilling The Promise**

God's fullness of time allows the events of history to ripen and come to flower so that God can use the time to good advantage. The prophet envisions God saying, "I will fulfill the promise I made to the house of Israel and the house of Judah." For a prophet, it was inconceivable that God would not fulfill a promise God had made. The Hebrew prophets emphasized the Hebrew belief that any promise God made was as good as fulfilled. One could safely trust any promise of God as being fulfilled right now. Because God had demonstrated God's faithfulness over and over again, one never had to question whether the promise would come true. "It was as good as done," the moment the word of promise was given. This is basic for how we view any word from God.

The word from God can be trusted, because God is the One who has given the word. We say about people whom we can trust, "He or she is as good as his or her word." About God we can say, "God is as good as God's word," and "God's word is as good as God." A good custom for worshiping families of the past was not to leave the Sunday morning worship service before the benediction. The tradition held that God's promise of providence and grace for the week was a promise God would keep. The sermon may be just so-so, and other parts of the service may not always be inspiring, but one can always trust the benediction or promise from God. This Hebraic concept of God's promise being a sure thing is more sure than anything else.

**At That Time**

What is sure is that God will opt for the right moment when God will deliver on the word of promise. God says, "In those days and at that time." For the prophet this meant that God chooses the zero hour, the time when things can and will converge to accomplish whatever God has in mind. The whole of history, the past, the present, and the future can be interpreted in the light of this fact. Our eternal God, who is timeless and lives beyond time, is willing to cross the dateline, lift the pages of the calendar, and set an alarm clock to meet the opportunity to manage the affairs of the day in favor of God's people.

Because God's actions at God's own discretion do determine the events of human life and all history, it is important for people to live accordingly. We can and should take the words of God seriously. Whether God is being revealed in law or gospel, we should be equally attentive to what God has revealed. In his case, the Prophet Jeremiah wanted to arouse the people of his day to what God could accomplish for them in the midst of their crises and depression. His word is a model for us as to how we should consider the promises of God in the time of tribulation and despair. This is especially helpful in our time when people express their frustration with local and world conditions. Regardless of how it is for everyone else, we know our own circumstances have a way of getting out of hand and leaving us depressed. Then it is good for us to recall how the prophet could be certain of how God works in our lives.

## A Righteous Branch

God's efforts in dealing with what happens in history are not relegated only for what will happen at the end of history. God works on the stuff of history in the here and now. The days and the time in which God acts are not postponements and delays as signs of God's immobility and indecision. Actually, God is moving, shoving, and pushing things along all the time. Much of the confusion that occurs in the world is the result of God's judgment upon what people are doing. Often we get that turned around. Sometimes we think that the people trying to frustrate the will of God are winning out. Often turmoil is the result, because God allows the machinations and doings of evil intent to bring judgment upon their own heads. The opposite is also true. God can interrupt the activities of people by breaking into history with the freshness and newness of the revelation of good will. That is the nature of the promise which Jeremiah wanted to hold out to the people of his time.

Jeremiah writes that God says, "In those days and at that time I will cause a righteous Branch to spring up for David; and he shall execute justice and righteousness in the land." The prophet could proclaim this in the face of the fact that he also had to tell them that they would see the city of Jerusalem laid absolutely desolate by the Babylonians. The people had resisted listening to that word. They had made Jeremiah a spy, accusing him of working for their enemy. However, the handwriting was on the wall. Judah would be destroyed. In spite of that, in due time the Righteous Branch would bring justice and peace to his people by revealing the blessing and healing the gracious word of God offers. In contrast to the power plays of the conniving enemies of the people and of God, from both within and without, the Messiah would grant peace and consolation to the people of God. The Righteous Branch, the Holy One of God, will share the irrevocable promise of God. The presence of the messianic figure will guarantee the good word the prophet delivers from God.

**For David**

Jeremiah pushes the promise further by reporting that God says, "I will cause a righteous Branch to spring up for David." The reference obviously is to what God had done for Israel through the servant King David. David had been that ideal king whom God had established upon the throne for Israel. David had been exemplary, because he had trusted the covenant God had made with the people. Because David had been this model, God had promised God would continue the line of rulers who would be able to rely upon God's goodness and providence through good kingly rule. It did not work out that way.

The succession of kings who followed David did not walk in his steps. The kingdom was divided, and monarchs in both the Northern and Southern Kingdoms failed to give a consistent witness to the gracious rule of God, which they were supposed to represent. During all of that time God sent prophets to remind the people how it once was and how it could be again. The prophets, like Jeremiah, were not afraid to deliver this word within the courts of the kings. Now Jeremiah said that God would restore the fortunes of God's people by sending One who would be a Second David, One who would resurrect the image of the king as God wanted the kings to be. In making that promise God demonstrated how God runs all of the past through a sieve to make it work for the benefits of the future. God had a painful memory of how poorly the kings had performed, but God had not forgotten the promise that God had made to David for the sake of the people.

**God Will Save**

The effect of God acting on behalf of God's people is that God's people will be preserved and be saved. "In those days Judah will be saved and Jerusalem will live in safety," says the prophetic word. We know God did preserve the people of Israel in the time of the Babylonian Captivity. The people also were brought back to Jerusalem and lived through the difficult time of the Restoration. The people managed to survive with the leadership of the Maccabees when the Hebrew faith was made illegal and the Temple was profaned. The Hebrew people have endured in spite of the many holocausts designed to destroy them. So also the Christian Church has survived periods of turmoil and persecution. The Christian community has also survived the threats to the faith from within that come from efforts to contort the message of grace by turning the gospel into law or by making church organization more important than the gospel.

In our own nation, where Christianity has had freedom to flourish in the past, some Christians feel uncertain about the future of the Church. The great pressures are not persecutions, but our affluence and the competing forces for the commitment of believers are serious problems for the church to deal with. In addition there is grave suspicion that political forces are working against the freedom Christians once enjoyed. Many Christians, too, are afraid that there are pressures for the Church to liberalize its own confessions and positions. If we take a breather, we can reflect on the fact that we have already survived much. We think of the 1960s as an era in which all major institutions, including the Church, were under severe attack. Or we can think of losing a whole generation of the Yuppies, who apparently now are making their way back into the Church. When given the opportunity to think about what we have survived, Martin Marty likes to quote a favorite professor who says, "We do not know enough about the future to be absolutely pessimistic."

**God Is Our Righteousness**

While it is true we would like to be somewhat optimistic about the future, when we look at the world and the performance of humanity, we cannot hope for a great deal. We know that the future is fraught with problems, pain, unbelief, and failure. At the same time the people of God can be more than just romantic or optimistic about the future. As the people of God we can be absolutely sure, because God has made the future days of promise for us. We know the prophetic word of Jeremiah was messianic. God did fulfill the promises he had made to the house of Israel and the house of Judah.

God sent the Branch of Righteousness, the Son of David, our Lord Jesus Christ, to save all of humanity.

Our Lord accomplished the fulfillment of God's promise by his death upon the cross and his resurrection from the dead. He executed justice and righteousness in a world filled with injustice, war, and unrighteousness. In him God justifies and gives us the gift of eternal salvation by the forgiveness of our sins. In so doing God imputes to us the righteousness of Christ. By faith we are saved, and Jeremiah's prophetic word proclaims we are now given that name by which we are called "the Lord is our righteousness." We cannot have it any better than that. Advent is the time for us to realize that we live in the days of rich promise which God has fulfilled for us in the sending of Jesus, the Infant of Bethlehem. We do that in a season in which the world will make the frantic effort to beat last year's or the best year's Christmas sales at the same time that it wonders if there is anything it can do to stop the murderous behavior in our metropolitan areas, solve problems of global warming, keep the peace in the Middle East, and solve social problems of drug and sex abuse so enormous one does not know where to begin. For us, though, Advent is that time when we can think seriously that the future holds great promise for us, because we know how God has fulfilled the promises God made in the past. These are days of promise for us, because God is with us.

*Advent 2*

# A Messenger Of Promise

*Malachi 3:1-4*

---

**A journal titled** *The Religion and Society Report* once editorialized that people are tempted to treat religion and society purely in terms of sociology or in terms of the politics of religion. The fact is that church bodies and ecclesiastical institutions are fair game for the sociologists who like to try to measure the churches as being either to the right or to the left. However, most sociologists are not in a favorable position to make judgments in that regard, because they do not understand that they are trying to chart a miracle. That was not the point of the editorial, however. The article noted that the Christian faith is occasion for the people of God to act as a community of faith, worship, and discipline which transcends the social and political categories of the world.

What we confess is far more important than the observable consequences of what we confess. Both the prophets and the apostles understood that. However, regularly journals and books appear insisting that we should be able to set things right in the society immediately and that the results should be measurable now. On balance, we have before us a prophetic word in which a messenger is promised who will turn things upside down. The prophet suggests that God would send the messenger of great promise. In these Advent days it is good for us to understand in what sense the messenger can hold out great promise to us.

### The Prophet

The name of the prophet who spoke or wrote the oracle that constitutes the First Lesson for today is unknown. The name

Malachi simply means "My Messenger." The Hebrew name was assigned the prophet on the basis of the lesson before us. This prophet carried on his ministry in the period of the Return of the people from the Exile in Babylon. He carried on this work before Ezra and Nehemiah.

The original intent of this word of promise was that God wanted to use his messenger to announce the return of the Presence of God in the Temple at the conclusion of the Exile. With that, the people could also be assured of the restoration of the Covenant that God had made originally with the people of Israel. Clearly, whoever collected these oracles of the prophet thought that the prophet who wrote or uttered them was the one to make these assurances real for the people. In time, the people were able to see the promises fulfilled with the rebuilding of the Temple. Yet tensions remained between the ideal and the reality. The religious community was to experience dark days in the future just as they had in the past.

**The Messenger Of The Covenant**

It is unlikely that the prophet who delivered this oracle saw its fulfillment. The editor who collected his oracles, or sayings, chose to amend the oracle by adding the thought that God would send Elijah as the promised prophet. Elijah, who stood tall among all the prophets, had been assumed into heaven. Elijah, therefore, could return to prepare for the great and terrible day of the Lord by turning their hearts to reorder their priorities (Malachi 4:5-6). Jesus knew of that tradition. His disciples once asked Jesus if he knew that Elijah must come to prepare all things. Jesus answered that Elijah had already come, had performed his duties, and had paid the price for the ministry of preparation (Mark 9:10-12). Thus it is our Lord himself who identifies God's messenger as John the Baptist.

In the Holy Gospel for today (Luke 3:1-6), John the Baptist is identified as the one whom the Prophet Isaiah predicted. As such, John is pictured as "the voice of one crying out in the wilderness." In either description of the messenger, he is to be the one who "prepares the way of the Lord." In either resumé the prophet who comes is also the one who works out of the covenant which God has established with God's people. Malachi says he is "the messenger of the covenant in whom you delight." This suggests to us that we must understand the message of the one who prepares the way of the Lord in the light of the covenant which God had long before established with God's people.

### The Message Of Change

The effect of what the messenger of change is to accomplish is considerable. The assurance is given that he will come. However, a question is raised as to who can endure his coming, because of the changes he will call for when he comes. Isaiah describes the coming of this messenger as a call for radically changing the landscape as an analogy of how people will have to be brought low in order the see the salvation of their God (Isaiah 40:3-5). The language in Malachi uses analogies of the refining of gold and silver and cleansing of fabrics in preparation for manufacturing. These analogies appear to suggest that the messenger comes with harsh words of judgment. Such thoughts would indicate that in order to set things right the messenger should use the power of the law to make sure everyone is worthy and well prepared to receive the God who comes to them.

The purifying language indicates that until the messenger is taken seriously the offerings the people make to God simply are not acceptable. The people should be enabled to "present offerings to the Lord in righteousness." Such talk sounds like a good deal of fire and brimstone preaching is called for to shake the people over the pits of hell to make them shape up. There are always a goodly number of preachers around willing to do that. The media are filled with messages from people trying to reform society from its drug culture, its violation of the environment, its violence, its wife and child abuse, its greed, and its disruption of the economy. Yet not much happens.

### The Heart Of Change

The failure of much social reform occurs because it is built on the assumption that the law can change people. The basic idea is that if you educate people as to how bad things are and show them how good they can be, they will opt for change and turn themselves around. The fact is that we very much do need the law to curb and shape behavior in the society. It is also true that we can accomplish much in social reform through education and counsel. However, what the messenger of the covenant works from is an entirely different assumption. The message of the one who prepares the way for God is far more radical. The change is to be far more than conformity to law or social standards. The change to be effected out of the covenant is totally dependent upon the efforts of God. The people who would prepare for the coming of God must be open to the fact that God himself must effect the changes.

God will use the messenger to do the refining and the purifying. The people cannot refine and purify themselves. The first admission we have to make is that we are not capable of changing ourselves. Because we are sinners, our attempts at reform will always come up short of what God requires of us in the covenant. However, as the covenant helps us to recognize our own inadequacy, the covenant also helps us to recognize that God made the covenant with the intent of helping us. Not only is God able to help us, but the covenant declares that we should have been totally dependent upon God in the first place. That we failed to rely upon God completely was not only our first error, but it is our persistent problem. Sin is our failure to understand that we are completely worthless without the help of God. That is what John the Baptist was preaching about when he preached a baptism of repentance for the forgiveness of sins. People needed to be immersed in the fact that they were totally undeserving sinners, but that they could also be bound to a forgiving God who wanted to give them hope.

**The Faith In The Change**

In these Advent days we are called to make the confession for which John called. We cannot hope to celebrate the Birth of our Lord at Bethlehem with any kind of meaning unless we understand that at our birth we were destined to be the children of wrath and condemnation. The days of Advent are designed to be days of contemplation of why God was willing to take the drastic action of making his only Son incarnate in order to make the sacrifice on the cross for our sin. God decided to take on this move, because there was not one human being in the whole wide world who could come up with an answer that would deal adequately with the depravity of humankind.

The messenger was to deliver a message of refining and purifying that is for the best. The act of purifying gold is a drastic action that brings good results. The dross is melted away in the hot fires of purification, but the result is the pristine metal of shining gold. So as we get through the first step of contrition, that is the act of giving up on ourselves, we are purified to permit God to make us what we should be. So also our repentance is likened to the fuller's soap that washes away the impurities of our sins and our selfish desires. What opens up to us in the covenant as we make ourselves candidates for listening to what God is willing to do for us is that God is believable. In the Person of our Lord Jesus Christ we can have faith that change is possible. That is what Dickens attempted to portray in his charming *Christmas Carol*. However, real change does not come by the Christmas ghosts, but by the Spirit of God who refashions us in the likeness of God's Son.

**The Change Is Service**

As the prophet saw the change happening in the people of God, he wrote that they would be able to "present right offerings to the Lord." The prophet viewed the tragedy that existed among his people. The excitement of the Return from Babylon had subsided. The city of Jerusalem was in ruins. The people languished. They were in their homeland, but they were not at home. The Temple was destroyed. The people who had remained in the city were a sorry lot. They were neither prosperous nor industrious. The returned exiles were disillusioned by what they found. They had no desire to build or do anything. In Babylon they saw their enemies prosper and witnessed what power and might they could boast. The people of Israel had to ask, "Where is the God of justice?" Nothing seemed to work out as promised. Consequently, there was great skepticism, and the people reflected their unfaith in bad behavior.

Worst of all, the priesthood had been unfaithful, and the priests were very careless in their practices. They offered polluted food on the altar and manifested general indifference to the needs of the people. It was the offering of polluted food (1:7) that was most offensive to God and a serious indication of how bad things were. The prophet was convinced that all this would change when the people were thoroughly cleansed through the work of the messenger of the covenant, who would bring the people to a sense of repentance and faith. Then conditions for the people of God would be as they once had been. Not only would the people bring right offerings to the Lord, but "then the offering of Judah and Jerusalem will be pleasing to the Lord as in the days of old and as in former years."

## The Change In Us

Justin Martyr, the foremost apologist for the Christian faith in the second century, described the Christian worship of the Church in one of his writings, *Apology 1*. He also described his understanding of the Sacrament of the Altar. He saw the prophecy of Malachi about the messenger as fulfilled in the Sacrament of the Altar, because he believed that Christians were able to make the perfect sacrifice. Not all Christian teachers agreed with Justin. We can agree only in the sense that we make the perfect sacrifice by faith. Actually God is the one who gives in the sacrifice as we receive the Christ who has died and is risen again. What we offer is ourselves as sinners, that we might be purified by our Lord Jesus Christ. Jesus is the one who has refined us and cleansed us with the fuller's soap of repentance.

By the Risen and glorified Christ we are set free to offer ourselves in what we do in our callings and vocations. Going back to our original observations about sociology, we have to ask who is able to measure what goes on in the change and the work of the people of God. Gunnar Myrdal, the Swedish scholar, gave us the landmark study *An American Dilemma*. He liked to think of sociology as social engineering, but he was quite disappointed in the directions that sociology took. He thought that sociologists should have behaved more as prophets who could call people to moral accountability. We can assert that not only do people fail at social engineering, but also they always will until they deal adequately with the kind of change the prophet called for with his word about the messenger. We do take the prophet seriously, and we are confident that this season of Advent is a precious time for us to renew our confidence in the kind of change God can perform in us anew. We can welcome any messenger of God who comes to us to share renewal in the light of the covenant of God's grace in Jesus Christ. We offer ourselves to be purified and refined as silver and gold that we may offer our lives to God in righteousness. Then we can properly pray, "Come, Lord Jesus."

*Advent 3*

# A Song
# Of Promise

*Zephaniah 3:14-20*

---

**In 1967** Shastokovitch, the Russian composer, wrote a symphony titled *October*. The work was to celebrate the fiftieth anniversary of the Bolshevik Revolution of 1917. In East Germany that year the Protestant Church observed the 450th anniversary of the Reformation. However, the dominant theme in East Germany that year was "Roter Oktober," "Red October," because of the dominance of the Russian government. The people were to celebrate their release from the yoke of Russian tsars and the freedom they had seized for themselves. What was meant to be freedom turned out to be a nightmarish era of oppression. One hopes a new era of freedom has dawned for the Russian people. However it will be, Shastokovitch's work will abide as a reminder of how the hopes of a people were spelled out in song.

Song as a medium of expressing hope and freedom, of course, is not new. "Yankee Doodle" was only one of many war songs to inspire Americans at the time of the American Revolution. During the Civil War in this country George F. Root wrote a sprightly tune for the Union troops. The tune was so catchy that a southern composer and a southern lyricist adapted it for the Confederate troops. Both sides boasted they were fighting for freedom. They gave voice to their hopes in song, and the tune was the same. In the First Lesson appointed for today the Prophet Zephaniah encourages the people of God to burst into song to herald the day of promise when Israel would once again be free.

## The Prophet

The Prophet who encourages this song in the hearts of God's people is the same prophet who had been a prophet of doom for his people. If the records are correct, Zephaniah was a Judean, born of royal blood in the latter part of the seventh century before Christ. A descendant of King Hezekiah, he probably was a cousin of the noble King Josiah. However, Zephaniah's role in the royal courts was that he came as a prophet. He sensed the calling of prophet when he regarded the invasion of Judah by the Scythians as a harbinger of a greater judgment to come.

Zephaniah sized up the condition of his people as ripe for judgment in the light of world events. He also envisioned "a day of the Lord" when all nations would suffer judgment from the wrath of God. Zephaniah could be specific about the enemies of Judah who would have to pay the price for their opposition to the people of God. All creatures, people and animals, in fact, everything on the whole face of the earth, would feel the full weight of this judgment. Judah would suffer, because Judah had engaged in the worship of idols. Judah had been guilty of violating the covenant relationship with the God who had created and redeemed Judah. None of these harsh judgments sounded like good reason for the people of God to join in a lusty song of praise. However the prophet also had another word for his people, a word of promise.

## The Remnant

While Zephaniah was absolutely convinced that Judah would have to pay dearly for her sins, the prophet also was convinced that God would be faithful to the covenant God had made with his people. The very nature of God is love. That love which God manifests in so many ways is also an assurance of God's faithfulness. God could never deny God's own self. That meant God could not withdraw from people the right to say, "No," to God. However, it also meant that God would never renege on the promises which God had made. God had revealed that God's word would never return void. There always would be some people who would respond in the affirmative to the overtures of love God had made toward the world.

Zephaniah could entertain notions of how utterly severe the judgments of God would be and are, but he also could affirm the goodness of God. In the light of what Zephaniah knew and could foresee, he also could determine that the number of people who would be faithful to God's word of promise would be very limited. The shrinking number, he determined, would be the "remnant." The remnant would be a core group of people who would be a minority both in the world and in the community of Judah itself. Zephaniah's successor, the Prophet Jeremiah, also learned to think of the faithful people of God as "the remnant." And that is the way it turned out. Though the group of people who consistently trusted God's promise was relatively small, they were the people who could be counted on to keep alive the promise of God for others to hear and trust.

**The Song**

Because no one could question or destroy the promise of God, the prophet could announce to all of Jerusalem that she should burst into song. "Sing aloud, O daughter Zion; shout, O Israel," the prophet could encourage. Anyone within earshot could act on this counsel and advice. All could trust that God would be the Savior and hope for all people living under the prospect of severe and divine judgment. The God who would deal judgment upon the whole world would remove the judgments on all who trust God. "The Lord has taken away the judgments against you, he has turned away your enemies." What judgment the world has stored up against itself, God would withhold from the faithful, the remnant in Jerusalem.

There was good reason for believers to break into song in the light of what God is willing to do for those who trust God. In the midst of threats and judgments, they could be upbeat. In the confusion and the chaos of the world, they could sing with melody in their hearts. Under the ponderous burden of defeat, they could chant a victorious battle hymn. They could chant festival songs when people felt the need to groan a funeral dirge for the world. God had created the melody for them with the promise of all that God was willing to do for their deliverance. Their history was the record of what God had already done for them. God had saved this people before, and God would do it again. The song would be a refrain of the songs of thanksgiving God's people had composed before.

**Songs Today**

The songs encouraged by the prophet are quite different from the songs of our age. So much of the contemporary literature composed for the symphony orchestras is dissonant, discordant, and harsh sounding. Composers have always been wary of imitating models from other periods lest they be regarded as being uncreative and lacking in originality. In the search for new expressions, the composers reflect the times in which we live. They portray for us the confusion and incongruities of our age by creating music that grates both on our ears and our emotions. It is no small secret that the conductors of great symphony orchestras of our land have considerable difficulty with their boards of directors when they include too many of the contemporary works in their scheduled concerts.

The same observations can be made about the popular music of the day. The complaints about the loud harsh music that is electrically amplified are not simply from an older generation that is out of sync with the younger. The questions are raised about music that it is totally unwholesome for the ears and may impair the hearing of young people at an early date. However, the more serious complaints are about music that also reflects a lack of morality and expresses only the more primitive passions of people. Besides complaining about loudness, the repetition, and the lack of artistry, one critic asked, "Why don't the songs have an ending?" The answer is that bad music has no soul to reflect a genuine and positive hope.

**A Special Song**

One certainly cannot characterize all contemporary music, popular or classical, as decadent or lacking in soul. There is much contemporary composition that is commendable. However, it is important to note that the prophet who called for a song from God's people did not look for them to express their sense of depression and lack of hope. He encouraged a song that would express divine hope in the midst of human confusion and terror. Martin Rinkart was such a hymn writer. Born in the latter part of the sixteenth century in Eilenburg, Germany, he received theological training and held several positions before returning to his home town as archdeacon. He served in that city for some thirty years, most of that time being during the Thirty Years War.

Because Eilenburg was a walled city, people from miles around sought refuge there. The overcrowding resulted in famine and pestilence. One pastor left and two died, leaving Rinkart to minister alone. He read burial services for as many as forty and fifty persons in one day. His wife succumbed to the pestilence, and he survived an illness. Rinkart received little support from the town authorities, and eventually was even harassed by them. Totally exhausted he went to his grave, December 8, 1649. What he bequeathed to us was not only his untiring example of unselfishness but his great hymn, "Now Thank We All Our God." In the midst of great tragedy and suffering he could offer the song of promise encouraged by the prophet.

**Always A Song**

Rinkart gave thanks in the midst of severe depression in the same way the prophet was confident that Jerusalem could break out in song in the face of devastation and annihilation. The Scythian hordes which had invaded Palestine were ruthless inhumane ruffians from the north comparable to the Huns at the time of the invasion of the Roman Empire. Yet, in the face of the worst, the prophet counseled the people to take heart, because the Lord, the King of Israel, was in their midst. They would not have to fear. Nor would they have to give up and let their hands grow weak. God was on their side, and God would give them the victory. The history of Judah subsequently appeared to belie that. Judah did go into captivity, and Jerusalem languished for a long time after the return from the exile. Yet there was that remnant of believers.

There was always that group of God's people who were cheered by the promises of God at the times of great hardship and trial. They were not daunted by the threats that hung over them. Out of the remnant came prophets, heroes, and leaders who kept alive the hope that God offered through the covenant promise. In the throes of great troubles, they could sing confidently "as on a day of festival." God was never at a loss to raise up someone or prompt someone to share that good word announcing God's presence and help for all who would accept God. Zephaniah set the stage for Jeremiah, that remarkable prophet who had to predict the doom of his people, witness the reality of it, and yet assure the people that God would once more rescue them from their punishment. God promised that he would "change their shame into praise," says the prophet. God promised to bring them home, to make them "renowned and praised" and "restore" their "fortunes." Thus the song went on in spite of the fact that there had appeared little to sing about.

**A New Song**

In the Advent Season it is customary for the Christian Church to sing the "Magnificat," the Song of Mary. The Evangelist Luke placed this song on the lips of Mary, the Mother of our Lord, when she visited her relative, Elizabeth, the mother of John the Baptist. The song celebrates how God turns everything upside down and makes everything right. Johann Sebastian Bach interpreted this great hymn in the beautiful cantata "The Magnificat." The one who gave real meaning to Mary's song was our Lord Jesus Christ. Jesus is the fulfillment of the promises of mercy which God had spoken to the patriarchs, to Abraham and his posterity. By his humble and impoverished birth Jesus gave hope to the world. The life, death, and resurrection of the One born in the ignoble conditions of Bethlehem assured the world that God is always present working to give us hope and make our hearts glad.

The world will be singing Christmas carols lustily again this year. The carols have been ringing out in McDonald's and Burger King since the first of December. The Christmas music expands and grows yearly to be the largest repertoire devoted to one subject in all the world. People want their songs to bring them joy in the season meant to create joy. Yet many of those songs are ditties with no message of hope or promise. The song of promise the prophet teaches us is one we can sing when there is nothing to be joyful about. The song of promise does not fall flat when a season ends. The song of promise does not fade when the Christmas trees are taken down and the holly and tinsel are removed. This is a song of real promise. The song of which the prophet wrote is the song the Holy Spirit impresses on our hearts to celebrate the goodness of God. The song holds out hope and gladness for us as we realize, in the prophet's word, that God daily "renews" God's love for us in Christ Jesus.

*Advent 4*

# A Town Of Promise

*Micah 5:2-5a*

---

**Sometimes little** towns, ordinarily only dots on the map, achieve great fame. Green Bay, a rural Wisconsin town, is notable because it sponsors a National League Football team. Bethlehem, Pennsylvania, was settled by Moravian Christians in 1735 to be a peaceful town of the simple life. The Moravians were descendants of John Hus, who suffered martyrdom for his faith in Bohemia before the Lutheran Reformation. The Moravians in Pennsylvania chose the name "Bethlehem" for their village, because they wanted to imitate the simplicity of life so apparent in the Christmas story. The headquarters of the northern province of the Moravian Church in America are still there. Ironically, the city is better known today as having been the center of what was one of the great steel companies of America, Bethlehem Steel. The name is an oxymoron, if there ever was one. The products of this company, which was associated with a name made synonymous with "little" by the Prophet Micah, proved to be a network of girders and framework for the expansion of this country.

The name of the original Bethlehem gained its fame from the Christmas story and the many fictional accounts of how our Lord was born there. Phillips Brooks, the famous preacher of the nineteenth century, immortalized the name of Bethlehem with the popular Christmas carol, "O Little Town of Bethlehem." Yet the significance and the importance of the town is best expressed in the message of the Prophet Micah, who understood what was to be involved in the divine choice of Bethlehem as the birthplace of our Lord, and why it was important for Jesus to be born there.

**Bethlehem Today**

The town of Bethlehem in Israel pops up in the news in our day from time to time. It has happened that the media has had to report the cancellation of Christmas celebrations in Bethlehem because of the kind of turmoil that continues in the Mideast. Local officials in the Bethlehem area do not hesitate to close down operations when they determine that terrorists are threatening acts of violence in the area. Those kinds of conditions are more normal than we should like to admit in our time.

When things are peaceful in the Bethlehem area, pilgrims are free to visit the Grotto of the Nativity and the Chapel of the Manger. The Church of the Nativity is reportedly the oldest church in Christendom. It was built by Constantine in 326 A.D. over the Grotto of the Nativity, the place where tradition has it that Jesus was born. The sites which have been and are favorites of Christian pilgrims exist amid the tensions that continue to be problematic in the Mideast. That, of course, was true of the area when Mary and Joseph came to the town under pressures from an alien Roman government. The situation was neither pleasant nor comfortable for them then. It was, however, the town of which the Prophet Micah had spoken with great promise many years before.

**Bethlehem's First Notice**

The first notice given the town of Bethlehem in the Scriptures is when Rachel, Jacob's wife, was lost in childbirth at the birth of Benjamin. Rachel died while the family was on the way to Bethlehem, and she was buried near there (Genesis 35:19). The town was also the setting for one of the most beautiful love stories ever written. Elimilech and his wife Naomi left Bethlehem with their two sons to go to Moab at the time of a famine. After the death of her husband and two sons, Naomi returned to Bethlehem with her daughter-in-law Ruth. Ruth married Boaz, a native of Bethlehem. Ruth became the grandmother of Jesse. Jesse had eight sons. The Prophet Samuel was sent to Bethlehem to anoint one of the sons as a future king. The son chosen was David, the youngest.

The three oldest sons of Jesse were conscripted into the army under Israel's first king, Saul. The sons of Jesse had to go into battle against the Philistines. David was still a young shepherd in his father's fields at the time, so Jesse sent David to carry some grub to his brothers. You know the rest of the story. David was soon engaged in the larger mission of a duel with the giant Goliath. David won that battle and gained favor in the eyes of King Saul, who enlisted him to serve in the royal court where he married the king's daughter and formed a deep friendship with Jonathan, the king's son. As Saul debilitated in his role as king, tension grew between Saul and David, and the two soon found themselves engaged in an unfortunate civil war. In a battle with the Philistines the desperate King Saul saw his two sons slain in battle and he committed suicide. David, fresh from a battle with the Amelikites, was anointed King of Judah by his troops.

**David As King**

From the beginning David was distinguished as an extraordinary person. He is known best for being a youthful victor over a giant. What was even more commendable is that he carried himself so well in his father-in-law's court. He had been of such an even temperament that he managed to preserve a faithful relationship with his brother-in-law Jonathan in spite of intrigue and foul play of the king. David was genuinely distressed at the death of Saul and took very seriously the appointment to be king.

What David accomplished in his administration as king was unique in the annals of the history of Israel and Judah. He merged the northern and southern provinces. He created a capital city at Salem to be known as Jerusalem. He extended the boundaries of his united kingdom and successfully warded off all challenges to the nation he believed to be the people of God. He was able to put down the civil war instigated by his own son, Absalom. He ruled with prudence, justice, and mercy. The secret of his success as an administrator, leader, and ruler was that he earnestly sought to live and rule by the covenant which God had made with the people Israel. When he ruled, he knew he had to serve as an agent of God. When he went into battle, he knew God was on his side. From beginning to end, he sought to have God rule through him and in him. When he sinned, he repented and served on in the freedom of God's grace and forgiveness. He knew that the throne belonged to God.

## A Second David

For Micah the promise of God that God would establish the throne of David forever among God's people meant that God would have to send another David. If God were to keep the promise to and for David, the one who would come to David's throne would have to be a clone of David. The king would be *David Redivivus,* "David Revived," or one who was like David in the manner in which David served the people. The new Davidic figure is not described in terms of the messiah so much as in the image of the *moshel,* a ruler. He is to be "one who is to rule in Israel, whose origin is from of old, from ancient days." That is to say, the new king is to be cast in the image of David to serve, as in the good old days, the welfare of the people of Israel. The prophet foresees the day when "the rest of his kindred shall return."

No longer would the kingdom be divided between the Northern and Southern Kingdoms as it was in the day of Micah, but the new David would be able to bring about the kind of unity the First David accomplished. Furthermore, the new David would also serve as a priestly king in the manner of David as "he shall stand and feed the flock in the strength of the Lord." In that respect the new Davidic figure will be most like the First David. However, because God sends the new David to keep the promise God made to the First David, God will increase what God has been doing for the people of God. Not only will the people be secure, but the Second David "shall be great to the ends of the earth."

## Who Says?

This hopeful word about a Second David coming to the rescue of God's people is contrasted with the record of David's successors to the throne. Both in the Northern and the Southern Kingdoms no one appeared to live up to the prophet's hope. God would have to start over. A Second David would have to come from Bethlehem to be "one who is to rule in Israel." Micah did not have trouble identifying with that thought. He was a rural peasant himself. He championed the cause of the peasantry which had been crushed under the tyranny and greed of the rich. The administration of the kings he knew had not been favorable to the people he loved. He also sensed that the fall of the Northern Kingdom of Israel was imminent.

Micah's view was rural and lacking in sophistication. He may have been regarded as a country bumpkin. Certainly the people had low regard of him when he suggested that the City of Jerusalem and the Southern Kingdom would also fall. To be sure, the fall of the Southern Kingdom was still a long way off. However, the prophet sensed that Judah could not prevail in her present practices without paying the price for her sins. The bold rustic prophet was, in fact, the first to predict the destruction of Jerusalem. The thought of the destruction of the holy city undoubtedly was as repugnant to him as to the people who believed that the holy city could never be assailed because God lived therein. A hundred years later Micah's prophecy was quoted in the royal court when people questioned Jeremiah's prediction of the city's destruction.

**He Was Right**

Micah was right. The Northern Kingdom did fall within a short period of time, and ultimately, Judah, the Southern Kingdom, fell also. The dreaded days the prophet had predicted became reality. At the same time those harsh prophetic judgments which fell on deaf ears had always been matched with the hopeful promises Micah had also written. If they fell on deaf ears, that was most unfortunate. Yet the thread of the promise God wove into all of history was discernable finally in the rich tapestry God wove with the life, death, and resurrection of God's Son, Jesus Christ, our Lord.

Jesus did prove to be the Second David of whom Micah wrote. The Second David brought unity to the children of this world who have faith in God through what Jesus had accomplished for them. All else the Prophet Micah had described concerning the Davidic figure matches the profile of our Lord. We can make an overlay of our Lord's career to fit the word from the prophetic text. It was not an accident that the Second David was born at Bethlehem. Clearly,

God did want to give the evidence that God was starting over with a descendant of David who would carry on what God had begun through God's faithful servant. Bethlehem's claim to fame was renewed. Not only had that rural village produced the likes of King David, but the town had given to the world the King of kings and Lord of lords.

**Our Bethlehem**

There was nothing provincial about the prophetic word from Micah. The Second David came to offer security to the world. The Christ affirms the prophetic word by feeding us from the very strength of God. He made it possible for us to trust God, because he won for us the forgiveness of sins by his death on the cross. He gives and renews life for us in God by his resurrection from the dead. He shares and offers all that through the Word and Sacraments. The Holy One who was born at Bethlehem is born anew for us at Christmas. The name of the town of Bethlehem means "House of Bread." *Beth* is "house." *Lechem* is "bread." This Christmas we celebrate at Bethlehem when we consecrate the bread at the Sacrament of the Altar.

As surely as God created God's Son to give him to the world at Bethlehem, each time we consecrate the bread of the Sacrament God gives God's Son to us. As Christ became incarnate as the Second David at Bethlehem, at the Sacrament, Christ is given again to us under the form of the bread. The Christ comes to us "housed" in bread. The kind of joy that filled the stable, or the cave, where our Lord was born awaits us as we come to the Lord's table. Shepherds at Bethlehem, where the First David had tended sheep, were invited to come and see the Second David in a helpless, homeless, and poor infant. The shepherds could see and realize this only through faith. So it is by faith that we come to behold him, knowing that it is because of him we can dwell secure. We do not have to wonder where our God is or what God is like. We know that God will feed us, just as David fed and cared for the people. We know where God is. God is right here at Bethlehem, our House of Bread.

*Christmas Eve/Day*

# The Child Of Promise

*Isaiah 9:2-7*

---

**Benjamin Britten's** cantata "St. Nicholas" is based on the legendary figure of Nicolas, Bishop of Myra. If Nicolas was truly an historical figure and the Bishop of Myra in Asia Minor, he would have been bishop in the latter part of the fourth century or the early part of the fifth century. Traditionally, Nicolas is the patron saint of sailors and children. The legends built around him are especially attentive to his care for the poor and helpless. He is noted for having spent his fortune on the poor and needy. Striking legends were soon attached to his person and ministry. He is reported to have calmed the sea during a violent storm, and the ship on which he sailed was saved. One story has it that he rescued three daughters of a nobleman who were about to enter upon a life of sin until he threw three purses in their window. No story is more famous than "Nicolas and the Pickled Boys." Three boys had been hacked to death by a butcher and thrown into vats of brine. Nicolas raised the boys who were able to sing alleluias to their king.

Mythical or not, Nicolas became a forerunner of the fabled Santa Claus remembered so much in our homes this Christmas. In the cantata, Britten has Nicolas chant his dedication of himself in service to God. The reason for offering himself, he says, is because he was moved by the terrible plight of humanity. He moans that he has found man "doomed to die in everlasting fear of death: the foolish toy of time, the darling of decay." The remarkable confession Eric Crozier, the poet for the Britten cantata, placed on the lips of Nicolas is a profound theological insight. The Prophet Isaiah would have us begin this night with a reflection on our condition when God decided to send to us a Son.

## Sitting In Darkness

When the Prophet Isaiah writes about "the people who walked in darkness," he means us. The prophet could cite all of humanity as being in the dark. That is what Britten meant in his cantata about humanity. When people live in the world on its own terms, they are "doomed to an everlasting fear of death" and are the chief "darlings of decay." If they fail to recognize the brutal facts about themselves and the world in which they live, they are the "foolish toys of time." For the moment in which he lived, the prophet meant the people who operated without the revelation which God is always willing to make for the sake of any people. We cannot be absolutely sure if Isaiah was talking about the revelation God was making with the enthronement of a new king in Judah, or if this was something to take place in the future with the enthronement of a king. It could also be that the prophet was thinking ahead to the time when an enthronement procedure would be followed in an inimitable way for a messianic figure who would resemble a regal Davidic figure.

In the light of what God has revealed in the person of the Holy Child at Bethlehem, we interpret what Isaiah was projecting for the people of his day as to be fulfilled in the person of Jesus. That is not to say that Isaiah did not have reference to a king enthroned in his day or one to be enthroned. However, what he does say about the revelation of God in a messianic figure was fulfilled in the person of our Lord Jesus Christ. What is important to note is that God makes this revelation for the sake of people who would otherwise be doomed to continue to walk in the dark. What this adds up to is that God was and is willing to reveal God's grace and goodness for the sake of all people at any and all times. Because we are included in the people of all times and all places being in the dark, we need to be alert to what God is doing for us when we contemplate anew the Birth of Jesus of Bethlehem.

**The Great Light**

The good news the Prophet Isaiah had for his people was that the revelation God makes for the people living in darkness is that God moves them into the light. He writes that the "people who walked in darkness have seen a great light; those who lived in the land of deep darkness — on them light has shined." It was Carl Sagan who did very much to popularize our understanding of the vastness of the creation and wanted so much our improved knowledge of the natural sciences to enlighten our general understanding and behavior in the creation. Mr. Sagan was born to a common home not likely to serve as an incubator for the sciences that occupied his entire career. However, as a youngster his curiosity about the lights in the heavens propelled him to pursue his scholarship in the sciences. Sagan's work, *The Demon Haunted World,* was a final bequest to us to warn against the superstitions, myths, and fables about the creation which haunt people. Dr. Sagan believed that science is the candle to offer light to put out the darkness created by false beliefs. We can be grateful for that. Luther would say that we should be thankful for all the scientists who help us to understand better the world in which we live. Luther would add we should bask in the light those learned people shine on us the same way the pigs, the cows, and the horses enjoy the same sunlight we enjoy.

However, the "great light" of which the prophet Isaiah writes is a light that is far more penetrating and meaningful than the important light of which Carl Sagan wrote. Isaiah means light in a much larger sense. This is the light that existed before the creation of light or the lights of the firmament. The "great light" is the revelation of God which is an enlightenment that enables us to see what the microscope and the telescope cannot reveal to us. Mr. Sagan would have limited his candle light to only what the sciences can establish as hard fact. Isaiah would see the larger light which illumines the hard facts of the perversity of human nature and the largeness of God's grace revealed in Jesus Christ. Those are not fables or superstitions. The perversity of the human condition underlies and underlines all of human history. The fullness of God's grace in Jesus Christ is written large in what happened in the life of that One who was willing to be born into the tempest of the human condition for our sakes. All of that is enlightening, and we cannot come to that purely by human reason. The light does not come on in the brightest of our own ideas that flash across our minds. The light comes from God. Jesus Christ is that Light.

**Joy For The People**

The Prophet Isaiah envisioned that the restoration of the throne of Judah with a faithful king would not only shed light on the people but would also bring joy to the people. He writes, "You have multiplied the nation; you have increased its joy; they rejoice before you as with joy at the harvest, as people exult with dividing the plunder." The prophet's description sounds like someone describing the glee of merchants at the successes of Christmas sales. A professor of history at the University of Massachusetts, Stephen Nissenbaum, made a study of the joys of Christmas with his famous research titled *The Battle for Christmas*. He noted that the courts in Massachusetts in 1659 had to declare the celebration of Christmas a criminal offense, because of disorder caused by the reveling, begging, and general marauding that went on in the season. The battle for Christmas has gone on ever since. No doubt the Christmas malls have done well again in assuring people that they could purchase the joy of Christmas for themselves and their families.

However, that most certainly was not the observation of the prophet. The prophet was speaking of the joy that comes to God's people when God rules again in their lives. For him that was the restoration of a Davidic-type king. For us that joy comes when we permit God to rule in our hearts through the Son God sent into history to be our Lord and Savior. Christmas joy is created in our hearts at the prospect of what The Babe of Bethlehem was and is capable of doing for us. What we come to celebrate each Christmas is the renewal of our understanding of what God has accomplished for us by the sending of this Holy Child.

**Facing The Enemies**

Isaiah trusted that the return of a Davidic figure upon the throne meant that the people of Judah would be able to come out from under the burdens of their oppressors. He believed that the new king would serve as David had done in being that warrior king who was able to do battle for the people and vanquish their foes, roll up their equipment in blood and destroy their war gear in fire. For us the Davidic king has come to enable us to conquer all that would oppress, stifle, and harass us. The Lord Jesus Christ came that he might deal with the problems of our guilt and shame before God. On the cross our Lord would die to sin, that we might know that God does not look upon us as sinners but as those who have been washed in the blood of the Lamb. All the charges and accusations which could be used against us are cast into the fire.

In the same way the little Lord Jesus who came to us at Bethlehem would grow up to be that true person who would live under God in perfect obedience that he might demonstrate for us and live for us a life that is living proof that God can be believed. There is no way in which Jesus modeled a perfect life of ease. Rather his life was filled with tensions, tribulations, and temptations and ended in anything but worldly success. "He was a flop at thirty-three," sings one ditty about him. In the same way that Jesus could trust God all the way from the manger to the cross, we can trust God through all our trials and tribulations from the cradle to the grave.

**The Son Is Given**

The wonder of what the prophet envisions in the sending of the Davidic figure to be the new king sitting upon the throne of God's people is that he could be regarded as a brother. This would not be an invading king, an alien king, an outsider. Rather, "A child has been born for us," says the prophet, "a son given to us; authority rests upon his shoulders; and he is named Wonderful Counselor, Mighty God, Everlasting Father, Prince of Peace." No one else fits this description by the prophet of a promised king as does the Holy Child of Bethlehem. Jesus is the one who in matchless ways and demeanor lived up to the kind of nomenclature the prophet chose to portray the One who came as a Second David to rule over all of humankind. He does not come simply as a king of Judah, a representative of God, but he is the Mighty God, who is the Wonderful Counselor, Everlasting Father, Prince of Peace.

What we celebrate this Christmas with special fervor is that the Mighty God, this Holy One who is Ruler over all, comes as the Holy Child. He has been born for us. He is a Son given to us. We can call him brother. In one of his Christmas cantatas Johann Sebastian Bach refers to Jesus as our *Bruederlein,* our "Baby Brother." Bach, who is one who understood the remarkable mystery of the incarnation, stated in the simplest terms the full impact of what God did in restoring innocence to humanity with the sending of this tiny brother to us. The full implication of what it was that he had to become our baby brother was that he might identify totally and completely with all that we have to face in the fullness of both life and death.

**His Authority Grows**

The prophet Isaiah was confident that the arrival of a Second David would ensure the growth of the people of God and endless peace for them. He wrote, "His authority shall grow continually, and there shall be endless peace for the throne of David and his kingdom." Once again, there is no evidence of that happening within the annals of the Kingdom of Judah, but we know by faith that this is what our Lord Jesus Christ, as the Second David, has accomplished. Our Lord has established a kingdom of love and grace that includes all nations and tribes and extends over all the earth as an offer of citizenship to all who would believe that a gracious and loving God has redeemed and saved the creation and all its creatures through the Christ of Bethlehem.

When the prophet speaks of the endless peace that the Second David would establish for the throne of David, he adds that the new King would "establish and uphold it with justice and with righteousness from this time onward and forevermore." What God had always intended that the throne of David should have been among the nations of the earth is now achieved throughout the nations of the earth by the Holy One, who sits at the right hand of the Father to rule over both heaven and earth until that day when he comes to judge all the nations of the earth in righteousness. What began so humbly and quietly at Bethlehem when God permitted God's Son to sneak into the history of humankind with the announcement by angels will come to that glorious climax when Jesus will return with all the holy angels to judge the world.

**It's All About The Son**

The Christmas Lesson taken from the Prophet Isaiah is well known to us all. It has been rehearsed for us in readings, songs, and prayers. What makes it so precious to us is the fact that so much is attributed to the person of that kingly Davidic figure who is our Lord Jesus Christ who comes to us as a Child. What is more important is that he is ours. We come this day to claim him again as our very own, and to have him as our own is to know and to have God in our hearts. One Christmas carol which captures that truth so poignantly is "Once In Royal David's City," sung with purity in the Service of Lessons and Carols each Christmas Eve in the King's Chapel at Cambridge, England. The third stanza of that hymn is particularly touching:

> *For he is our childhood's pattern,*
> *Day by day like us he grew;*
> *He was little, weak and helpless.*
> *Tears and smiles like us he knew:*
> *And he feels for all our sadness,*
> *And he shares in all our gladness.*

In the Holy Child of Bethlehem not only the joy of Christmas is ours, but also he gives us joy to all eternity. Amen.

*Christmas 1*

# The Promising Child

*1 Samuel 2:18-20, 26*

---

**The Holy Gospel** appointed for this First Sunday after Christmas was chosen to help us understand the development of that Holy Child whose birth we have just celebrated with joy and high delight. However, in Bible classes pastors generally have difficulty handling the protests of mothers who think that the behavior of the twelve-year-old boy Jesus was quite reprehensible. Mothers normally contend that no matter how impressive Jesus may have been with the teachers in the Temple, he gets poor marks for the anxiety he caused both Mary and Joseph. Any parent who has experienced the trauma of worrying about a lost child for any length of time can appreciate the fact that Mary immediately faulted Jesus for what appeared to be thoughtlessness on his part in not informing his parents of his whereabouts.

We can be sure that the Evangelist Luke did not intend to portray Jesus in such a bad light. In fact, the evangelist relates the story to inform us of the faithfulness of both the parents and the Child Jesus. In an earlier story Luke recounts the Presentation in the Temple when Mary and Joseph carefully fulfilled all that was required of them according to Hebrew law and tradition. In the Gospel today Luke reminds us that Mary and Joseph went to the Passover festival in Jerusalem each year. Normally, that was required only of the adult male in the family. However, this pious couple went together each year, and, no doubt, took Jesus with them. That would also account for the fact that Jesus felt comfortable in what he was doing. To appreciate fully what was going on between Jesus and his parents we can look to the First Lesson appointed for today, the story of Samuel and his mother Hannah. The Evangelist Luke found this to be a model for his treatment of the accounts of the infancy and childhood of Jesus.

**About Hannah**

The story of Hannah is one of the accounts from the Hebrew Scriptures that is well-rehearsed in the Church. Hannah was the beloved wife of Elkanah, a man from Ephraim who had two wives. Hannah was barren, but the other wife of Elkanah, Penninah, did have children. Each year Elkannah took his entire family to worship at the temple which was at Shiloh. At whatever festival the family was celebrating they had a special feast, and Elkanah would present gifts to each member of his family. Out of love and sympathy for Hannah, her husband gave her double portion of the gifts. Yet Hannah was not consoled. She refused to eat and went to the temple and prayed through tears for God to bless her with a child. In her prayers she vowed to God that were she to be blessed with a son, she would dedicate the child in service to the Lord.

Eli, the priest, observed Hannah in prayer and thought she was drunk, because she moved her lips but did not speak audibly. The priest reproached her for her behavior, but she explained that she was not drunk. She also revealed her distress and why she had been praying in such a state of anxiety. Eli dismissed her with a blessing with the hope that God would grant her petition. She returned to her family, ate of the festival foods, and returned to her home with joy. Her prayer was granted, and she bore a son whom she named Samuel. When Elkanah took his family again to Shiloh for the annual worship, she preferred to remain home with the child. She waited until she had weaned Samuel and then took him and an elaborate sacrifice to present Samuel to the Lord. She explained to Eli that she had been the woman he had comforted, and now she was placing the child in Eli's care that the child might live a life of service to God.

**Lent To The Lord**

When Hannah placed Samuel into the care of Levi, she said, "For this child I prayed; and the Lord granted me the petition.

Therefore I have lent him to the Lord; as long as he lives, he is given to the Lord" (1 Samuel 1:27-28). The Law of Moses (Exodus 13:1-2) did require that every firstborn male be designated as holy to the Lord. The understanding of this requirement was that Israel might trust that God claimed all of Israel as God's people. The dedication of the firstborn was a significant way of remembering that, especially since all the firstborn of the Egyptians were lost at the time of the Exodus. Hannah and Elkanah went well beyond that in offering their very young son to serve the Lord for all of his life.

Many of our Christian families had such traditions among them. The Irish Catholics who came to America were noted for their willingness to offer one of their sons to serve as a policeman, one in some political office, and one in the priesthood. Anglicans were noted for offering a son to government service, another to banking, and one to the Anglican priesthood. In German Lutheran homes it also was common practice to offer a son to the ministry. In rural areas the joke often was that the one who was not strong enough for working the farm should go to the ministry. In the case of Roman Catholic and some of the German Lutheran families, this meant that the young boys were enrolled in pre-theological and liberal arts training schools at the tender age of twelve or thirteen. The difficulty of the separation from mother very often was equally traumatic for the young boys, and the good plan sometimes had to be aborted.

**The Faithful Mother**

It is not difficult to understand that when a mother offers her son for service to the Lord that this is done with mixed feelings. On the one hand, the mother, like Hannah, is prompted by the highest motives and sincere devotion to God. That must be not only with a sense of offering one's best gift but also with thanksgiving and proper pride that one is able to do so. The Hannah story exudes that kind of joy. At the same time, any time a mother must experience separations from her children she has a deep feeling that is incomparable with any other kind of loss. She senses a pain of separation when her children go to kindergarten for the first time, when they move on into the freedom and confusion of adolescence, when they marry, and, worst of all if they should precede her in death. If we can understand that, then we can appreciate the feelings of Hannah and the mothers like her who dramatized the separation of their sons from their sides when they offered them for service to the Lord.

While we can imagine the farewell of Hannah for the boy Samuel may have been a bittersweet kind of experience, the writer who gives us the account of that moment does not describe Hannah's feelings. Instead the writer simply states, "She left him there for the Lord." Then the writer includes a beautiful psalmody we know as "The Song of Hannah," in which her faith in God is described as a thanksgiving for all that God had done for her in granting her the gift of her son Samuel. She regards this as a victory of faith. The song goes on to praise God for the manner in which God reverses the fortunes of the poor and lowly and humbles the proud. The song, which became a model for the "Magnificat," the song of Mary at the time of the Visitation recorded by the Evangelist Luke, celebrates God's control over all of life.

**The Blessed Mother**

In the First Lesson appointed for today we read that Hannah faithfully made the annual visit to the temple at Shiloh to worship. As she did so she also visited with her son Samuel and brought him a linen ephod which she lovingly and carefully fashioned for him each year. The ephod was a liturgical garment. It was a light garment that covered only the front of the body. As an apron-type garment it was meant for service in the temple and designated the wearer of it as a servant for the worship ceremonies. No doubt, she took pride in her handiwork but was all the more proud of her son Samuel as he performed his duties and functions in the house of the Lord. By the same token, Samuel must have been equally proud and grateful as he wore the ephod as a symbol of the presence of his mother's love and care as well as her devotion to God.

In addition to the mutually rewarding experiences Mother Hannah and her son Samuel had from the satisfactions of their joint commitment of service to God, Hannah had other blessings. Each year as she worshiped at Shiloh the priest Eli would bless both Hannah and Elkanah. He made a ritual of saying to them, "May the Lord repay you with children of this woman for the gift she made to the Lord" (2:20). Those blessings became realities in the life of Elkanah and Hannah. Hannah was blessed with the gifts of three more sons and two daughters. In the meantime Samuel continued to mature and grow in his role as the servant of the Lord. One gets the impression that Hannah felt especially blessed in her role as a faithful mother.

**The Blessed Family**

The beauty of the Hannah Story for all of us is clearly how the faith of a wife and mother was not only for her personal benefit. She was to influence the lives of many through her son Samuel. As in the stories of Sarah and Abraham and Zechariah and Elizabeth, sons born are born to barren women. By God's grace and providence, the sons born to these barren mothers are ordained to be special servants of God and unique individuals. Though he was not born to the priesthood, Samuel was dedicated to the priesthood in a special way and, in addition, distinguished himself to become a judge and a prophet in Israel. Samuel was to be a shining reflection of the faith and godliness of his mother. From his youth on he was distinguished as being a man of prayer, just as his mother was immortalized by the fervent prayers she offered to God. Samuel stood tall among men as a man of faith. We can only guess, but we can imagine that Hannah was an equally good mother for all of her children and that they also mirrored her goodness in their lives.

We could only guess as to how many times the story of Hannah has been repeated in the lives of outstanding figures in history who would pay tribute to the mothers who bequeathed their faith to them. John Wesley's mother was dubbed the "Mother of Methodism," because of her noted faith and executive abilities which she passed on to her sons John and Charles. Probably one of the best known mothers in America is Abraham Lincoln's mother, because of his famous tribute to her, "All that I am, or hope to be, I owe to my angel mother." However, we do not have to recite the lists of prominent historical figures to make the point that the high and the mighty are indebted for their success to good mothers. The story is repeated every day in the homes of good God fearing people where mothers bequeath their love and faith to their children in constant faithfulness. The world continues to stand, and history moves on, because God can rely on these dear mothers to do the divine work of raising God's children.

**The Blessed Son**

The purpose of reviewing the story of Hannah and Samuel on this day was to help us appreciate the story of the Boy Jesus in the Temple. In the light of the story from the Hebrew Scriptures we can understand why Jesus answered as he did his very anxious Mother Mary when she remonstrated with him about his dallying in the Temple. The Evangelist Luke, who used the Hannah story to model the accounts of the Visitation and the Presentation, would also use Samuel as the model here. Jesus had good precedent for remaining in the Temple in the person of Samuel, who had entered the service of the temple at even a more tender age than Jesus. Luke indicates that at the moment neither Mary or Joseph understood what Jesus was saying to them. We understand. We understand, because we know the rest of the story. We know how Jesus lived out his life under the Father by his life, ministry, suffering, death, and resurrection. Knowing that, we can imagine he could have said anything he wanted to his Mother Mary. But he did not.

The Boy Jesus did not say more or less than he did, because he still needed to mature, to grow up, and to deepen his own understanding of what he himself had said. Luke adds, "He went down with them and came to Nazareth, and was obedient to them ... And Jesus increased in wisdom and in years, and in divine and human favor." Jesus needed the continued faithful love, instruction, care, and rearing of his beloved mother. The Story of the Boy Jesus in the Temple is included by the Evangelist Luke so that we can understand how dependent Jesus was upon the love of Mary and Joseph in a truly God-fearing home. It was in that home Jesus experienced the love and grace of his Heavenly Father. That is how it should work in all of our homes. God does reveal the divine to us in this homely way. And we are blessed.

*Christmas 2*

# The Children Of Promise

*Jeremiah 31:7-14*

---

**A serial killer** is the object of a serious psychological study in the novel *The Alienist* by Caleb Carr. The alienist in the nineteenth century was an expert in mental pathology. In this story, set in 1896, the alienist is Llazo Kreizler, hired by Theodore Roosevelt, then Commissioner of the New York City Police Department. Mr. Roosevelt was intent upon apprehending the serial killer of the young boys caught in the web of an unsavory lifestyle. As Kreizler tries to develop a characterization of the nature of the killer, a woman on his handpicked staff suggests that the primary clue to understanding this warped personality is that he had been abused by or totally rejected by his mother. At first Kreizler ignores the suggestion. Later he has good reason to capitulate to the suggestion, and the idea becomes an important factor in discovering the killer. The novel is historical in its setting, and is remarkably well constructed and written.

Mr. Carr has rendered us a service in helping us to understand that the perversity of our generation is not new. Furthermore, the novel strongly suggests that our present struggles to assist and strengthen the family are vital to the health of our society. The Lessons appointed for this Second Sunday after Christmas indicate that, in spite of the universal perversity of humanity, we are capable of being saved and enjoying great security as the children of promise. The Holy Gospel relates how we have power to "become the children of God." In the First Lesson the Prophet Jeremiah explains the blessings of the children of God. What Jeremiah has to say is important for us as the children of promise.

## The Context

Jeremiah would appear to be the least likely of the prophets to say anything encouraging about Israel as the people of God. We do not know much about the personal lives of most of the prophets, but we do know enough about Jeremiah to realize just how unpopular he was. He was not understood by his colleagues, and the people in general did not appreciate him. Commonly, he was regarded as being a wild crusader who was not going to serve the welfare of his people. Because Jeremiah sensed that the people of Israel were under judgment for their indifference to the covenant God had made with them, he knew the signs were present which indicated Judah would be overrun by the Babylonians and carried into exile. He preached the warning about Judah's imminent fall. The people believed Jeremiah wanted that to happen. The people suggested Jeremiah must be on the side of the Babylonians. The princes opposed him, and the temple guard Pashur had Jeremiah arrested. However, no legal action or imprisonment could keep the prophet from preaching what needed to be said as a clear revelation from God.

It was not out of hatred or revenge that Jeremiah was teaching what he did. However, the prophet could not deliver what was popular or what the people wanted to hear. The prophet was not called to entertain the crowd or fill them with optimism about their future. Faithful to his calling, Jeremiah consistently called the people to repentance and made the effort to help the people understand the judgment that awaited them. This was not easy for Jeremiah. There were times he himself was bitter towards God and wondered why his people could not get a better break. In those moments he was not disgusted with the civil or ecclesiastical leaders or the people. At those times he was disgusted and discouraged that God could not make the situation right with some kind of fiat. He had believed that God's word would be effective among the people, but he just could not see the good results.

## God Does Save

Jeremiah's bitterness resulted from his feeling of being deceived by God. He had thought that when he accepted the office of prophet that things would go well. The people should have responded affirmatively by believing. However, the people did not. Yet why should God be picking on these people when the other nations were even worse that the people of Judah, and they appeared to be prosperous and powerful? How come? The answers were obvious. Other nations also will ultimately suffer the judgment of God. However, for now the people of Judah were the ones who should have known better. They had the covenant of God. They had been chosen of God to be especially blessed. Jeremiah had begun his ministry during the reign of Josiah, a faithful servant of God, who had instituted temple reform. Unfortunately, Josiah had made a bad military judgment and was killed in battle by Pharaoh Necho and his Egyptian army at the Battle of Meggido. Josiah was succeeded by his son Jehoiakim, who ruled as a puppet of Necho.

Jehoiakim was cruel, selfish, sensuous, and totally ineffective as a king. During the reign of Jehoiakim the people suffered from the lack of leadership, and they had become perfunctory and indifferent in their religious life. Jeremiah felt deeply for these people, and he also sensed how God felt about them. God would never give up on them. God would save them. Jeremiah had all these feelings swelling within himself. He was angry with the people for not believing, yet he loved them. He was still bitter towards God for the judgment on Judah, and yet he sympathized with God's predicament. He hated himself for what he had to do, but he knew he had to do it. It was the word, the word of God, that guaranteed it would all come out right. The word said in God's own time and God's own way God would save and redeem God's people. In spite of all of his own feelings, Jeremiah knew God would not renege on God's earlier promises

**God Gathers**

The prophet could proclaim, "Hear the word of the Lord, O nations, and declare it in the coast lands far away; say 'He who scattered Israel will gather him and will keep him as a shepherd a flock.' " Israel's exile to Babylon should not be regarded as happenstance. Israel would have to pay the price for not having regarded the covenant God had made with Israel. It was God who would scatter Israel and uproot this people from their place among the nations. Israel could not afford to ignore the offer of God's providence and grace. To live apart from the rule and dominion of God, would be to suffer life without the benefit of God's protective arm. That would result in the scattering of Israel. Israel would be scattered because God had not only allowed them to be carried into exile, but had also arranged history so that when people ignore the offers of God's grace they must accept the fate that others will deal them. The enemies can take over.

At the same time God is not indifferent to the promises and offers God had made in the past. As surely as God had scattered them, God would also gather them. This was the good word the prophet could offer. Not only would God see to it that they would be able to return home, but God would also attend them like a shepherd tends his flock. We know how our Lord Jesus Christ seized on this model of God's care for God's people. Jesus identified himself as the Good Shepherd. When Jesus did that, Jesus was not introducing a new idea. Rather, Jesus drew on the shepherd models in the Psalms, the Prophets Jeremiah and Ezekiel, and the Hebrew tradition that could find comfort in God's behavior toward them as the Shepherd God. The prophet explained briefly what that meant, God "will keep him (Israel) as a shepherd a flock." Jesus explained that further as the Shepherd giving his life for the sheep.

## God Ransoms

Shepherding the people of God involved more than bringing them from the far flung corners of the earth to reinstall them in Jerusalem. The prophet continues, "For the Lord has ransomed Jacob and has redeemed him from hands too strong for him." A homecoming is exciting in itself. However, to recover from what has happened in a strange land is not easy. In America we know how painful the process has been when our people in the services have returned home after fighting in war. The social and economic pressures have been difficult enough for servicemen returning home from the wars. Our most recent memory of how difficult that can be was with our people who served in Vietnam. Many returned when their fellow service people were still in 'Nam. Most had seen the worst of the terrors of war. They returned to see their fellow citizens living in protest of the war they had fought. They returned to an economy that did not treat them well and in many cases left them jobless. They returned with an appetite for the drugs that had eased their struggle with an awful war. All of them returned shocked by the kind of inhumanity that war introduced to history. Like the scars of war, Jeremiah knew his people would bring deep wounds from their exile.

Jeremiah knew that some exiles would be maimed by blindness and lameness, but all would be weeping. The tragedy of it all was that they realized that they had been overcome by a world power, the "hands too strong for" them. They had to be humbled in this way to discover their dependence upon the God who had chosen them to be a special and unique demonstration of God's care for people. They would be but a remnant of Israel, a number greatly dwindled from a nation God had sought to make large in the family of nations. They would be but a shadow of their former glory, but they could be sure they were still God's people. "For," God says, "I have become a father to Israel, and Ephraim is my firstborn." God could never forget the promise God had made and protected from the day God first called Israel in the wilderness.

**They Shall Repent**

The remnant who experience the return from exile by the hand of God will be repentant. However, their repentance will appear differently than we normally expect. Usually we think of people groveling in the dust and ashes as they mourn over their sinfulness and renounce their stubbornness. This time, however, the repentance obviously would be different. It was not as though the remnant had no sorrow for their sins. This people will have had their days of mourning and sorrow for their rebelliousness and their indifference toward God. They will have paid a price in their exile, but they also will have been brought low to acknowledge their sinfulness. Then followed those days in which they were sorrowful because they were sure that God could not nor would not forgive them for their folly of unbelief. They were to have long periods in which they were sure that they would have to spend the rest of their days in repentance and sorrow for what had happened to them. They could also read the signs of the times as indications they would never gain the strength on their own to break out of their exile and return to their homeland. The prophet, however, saw otherwise.

Though the prophet scored the people for their apostasy, he could also encourage the remnant to look forward to that time when they could sing songs of gladness and raise shouts of joy. Their repentance would take the form of strong assurances of hope and confidence that God was in their midst to work their redemption as the people of God. Now their sorrow will be turned into gladness, their mourning into joy. The sign of their repentance is that they would have hope when there would be no apparent reasons for them to have hope. They will believe that they were going home when there was no announcement of a deliverer on the scene. But they would know who the Deliver is. He who had scattered Israel would gather them and keep them as a shepherd keeps his flock. God would behave toward them as God had acted on behalf of the people of Israel from the beginning.

**A Time For Joy**

One can understand why this pericope, or lesson, was chosen for this Second Sunday after Christmas. All the prophetic encouragement to engage in songs of joy and gladness fits this season when we recognize what God has done for us in the Person of our Lord Jesus Christ. Jesus took on the role of the Good Shepherd when he came to be our Savior and Redeemer. Jesus referred to himself as the Good Shepherd. He used the illustrations of the work of the Good Shepherd to explain what he would accomplish for our salvation. When God did return the remnant, the exiles in Babylon, to Jerusalem, God used an alien king of Syria to serve as their benefactor. The king not only released them from their captivity but granted them safety on their return and allowed them to take with them the sacred vessels that had been taken from the Temple. However generous Darius proved to be, the role of Good Shepherd belonged to God, who used the king for his purpose, which God continued until the sending of God's Son, who would be the incarnation of this role of Good Shepherd.

We know the role of Good Shepherd cost Jesus of Nazareth his life as he laid down his life for the sheep. However, the prophet did not ask the remnant to count the cost God would have to pay to move them out of exile. What he asked them to do was to look to the word of the Lord, trust what God had promised and know that he would deliver them. That is what we are called to do in this Christmastide. As we look to what God has done in the sending of God's Son in human form to be laid in a manger, we cannot think of the Child without reflecting on the fact that the Christ is destined to be nailed on the cross for our sakes. Yet in this Christmastide we are called to that kind of repentant faith that rejoices and exults in the fact that the Holy Child is the most holy and dearest sign of God's grace and love for us.

**We Celebrate**

There are times in our lives when we are encouraged to cheer up. Sometimes those times come when it appears as though there is nothing to cheer about. We think of how difficult it is to keep a stiff upper lip, let alone rejoice when the family has suffered the loss of a dear one. We know how hard it is to be cheerful when we have had a bad report from the doctor on the outcome of our checkup. We cannot deny our feelings of grief or pain at those times. However, what the prophet could say in the worst of times and what our observance of Christmastide holds out to us is that we can break out of our hurt and suffering to celebrate the goodness of God. Christmas comes each year when darkness settles so heavily upon the creation. We try to offset that with the blaze and gleam of our Christmas lights. However, the news of the world, local, national, and international, always reflects the trauma of the human condition.

It is important for us to celebrate the goodness of God in the midst of the worst news from the world. Pastors often have difficulty making appointments with shut-ins in order to commune them. A frequent answer is, "Not today, Pastor. I'm not feeling well." At that time the pastor can offer that this is when the shut-in needs the pastor the most. It is then that the pastor can offer the rich consolation of the gospel. We are equipped with the gospel to bring consolation at the darkest of times. The prophet says, "I will give the priests their fill of fatness, and my people shall be satisfied with my bounty." The people of God have every reason to sing aloud and to be "radiant over the goodness of the Lord."

*Epiphany*

# The Promise Of Sight

*Isaiah 60:1-6*

---

**The Epiphany** of our Lord never fails to arouse fascination for the story of the Visit of the Magi. The number, the identification, the homelands, and the occupations of the men from the East are not cited in the biblical account. That has allowed for all kinds of speculation as to who and what the Magi may have been. Some of that has been scholarly, some playful, some artful, some of it educational, and some worshipful. Carlos Menotti relates how fortunate it was for him that he could fall back on the traditional lore of his native Italy when he was called upon to produce the first opera created for national television, *Amahl and the Night Visitors*. He remembers the pressures he felt for making deadlines for the performance of the opera. He would have been in difficult straits were it not for the fact that his mind filled up with fond remembrance of the names and characterizations of three regal figures whom he made come alive for his operatic production.

One could add to Mr. Menotti's experience the numberless short stories, tales, novels, and art which have been created about the Magi in much the same way. Much of what has been created or written about the legendary figures has been full of charm and warmth, but the larger portion of what has been piled up has cast little light on the revelation of the Holy Child to the foreigners from alien countries. However, the text chosen from the Prophet Isaiah for the observance of this important day in the liturgical calendar offers much for understanding Epiphany. Doubtlessly, the reading was chosen because of its inclusion of people and camels who came from afar with gold and frankincense representing foreign nations. However, the text also has a great deal to say about the light that was shed on the world by the Epiphany, or the Manifestation, of our Lord.

**The Context**

One cannot say enough about the courage and conviction of the Prophet Isaiah, who penned the words of our text. This Isaiah was the prophet who ministered to the people of Israel while they lingered in captivity in Babylon. This ministry probably took place about 550-540 B.C. and broke through the gloom that had settled upon the previous generation of Hebrews. Israelites realized for a long time that they were a banished nation which had lost its identity as a people of God. Their capital city, Jerusalem, lay in ruins. Their national shrine, the Temple, had been desecrated and destroyed. They had lost their place under the sun and in the family of nations. That was humiliation enough. What was more frustrating was that their own history had been so bumpy and disappointing.

If the Israelites knew their own traditions, they knew their forefathers had been delivered from slavery before in the land of Egypt. Their tradition was filled with stories of how they conquered a land they assumed had been given them by divine promise. The breakup of their own nation had occurred once before when they had been conquered and taken into exile. The captivity of the Northern Kingdom had taken place a whole century before. The whole history of this people extended backward 1,300 years. How much the average Hebrew exile may have known about Hebrew history is difficult to say. We can imagine their sense of history was just as dim as what the average Christians know about their tradition of two thousand years. That is what the prophet had to overcome. The people had to be reminded of what God had done for them throughout their history to understand that God could again save them.

**The Light**

In order to inspire his people with the hope that was theirs in the gracious God who had not abandoned them in the exile, Isaiah composed effective poems about the favored position of God's people. He begins the poem before us, "Arise, shine; for your light has come and the glory of the Lord has risen upon you." When the prophet speaks about the light, he refers to that light which the Scriptures consistently identify with the presence of God. The prophet does not mean that the people should bask in the sunshine of the creation and glory in what the creation itself reveals about the providential Creator God. This light is the light that emanated from God at the creation before God created the luminaries of the creation. This light is the light that God shines into the hearts of people for them to see everything in a different light.

The prophet can say that darkness covers the earth "and thick darkness the peoples." The people of the world who do not know the God of the prophet are in darkness no matter how much they know and how much they have perceived about the world. The prophet says that this light dawns on people as the Lord "rises" upon them and God's glory appears over them. That is the light of which we speak in the Epiphany of our Lord. As a unique light led the Magi to find the Holy Child, so God enlightens us so that we can embrace the Child as the Son of God and Savior of the world. The faith that makes such identity possible is a gift from the light which God sheds upon our minds and hearts as we are captivated by the story of the Almighty God revealing the divine presence in the birth of an infant Boy.

**A Reunion**

For the prophet the presence of the Light which emanates from God would enable the exiled Israelites to be reestablished as a people of honor among the family of nations. He envisioned, "Nations shall come to your light, and kings to the brightness of your dawn." Once more the people could think of themselves as that nation in whom other nations of the earth would be blessed. The other nations would be blessed, because Israel would once again be the depository of that revelation in which God would offer demonstrations of how God could and does work history. Other peoples could learn how God does love, redeem, and save those who would trust God's willingness to help them. All this would be obvious in the manner in which God would bring home the exiles from Babylon and restore them again with those people who had been left behind in Jerusalem and also with the many who had been scattered around the world. The prophet writes, "Lift up your eyes and look around; they all gather together, they come to you, your sons and your daughters shall be carried on their nurses' arms."

The many Jews who had been dispersed throughout the Mediterranean world would be able to return to the Holy City of Jerusalem to celebrate the great festivals which honored the mighty acts God had performed in the history of this people — a people that had not only been demoralized but had also been decimated and separated by the world powers that had run over them, because they were a weak and vassal state. Weak administrations in Judah had made compromises with growing world powers, and had made unholy treaties and pacts, but failed in both their diplomatic efforts as well as their attempts at military alliances. Now, however, God would make them a people again with no military hero, no great political figure, no creative governmental enterprise of their doing. In spite of their ineptness at the conference table or on the battlefield, God would raise them up to be God's people again.

**The Prophetic Task**

In order to appreciate the task that Isaiah had in rousing the exiles to trust that God was still in their history, imagine what the rabbis have to do for the Jewish people today after the holocaust. It is one thing to know that generally people should be horrified at the inhumanity that took place with the slaughter of six million Jews. All people should be revolted at that horrible moment of history. Certainly there are segments of the Hebrew population who react to the holocaust only on its humanitarian and political levels. However, the rabbis have to interpret this dreadful catastrophe in the light of their own tradition. A remarkable collection of what some rabbis did teach in response to the Holocaust has been published under the title *I Will be Sanctified*. One rabbi noted that the question, "Where was God during the Holocaust?" is the question of those who would justify giving up on the faith of their tradition. Some would ask the question in pain, some ask out of sincere doubt, and still others ask insolently and skeptically. However, the one who questions out of faith is like the one who asked his young nephew, a survivor of the Holocaust, if he had seen the smoke coming from the chimneys. But then he also asked, "And did you see God there next to the chimneys?"

Faith not only recognizes the judgment of God upon the world, but also recognizes the willingness of God to save and redeem out of the worst of circumstances. That is what the Prophet Isaiah was able to see and what he was able to share with his people in exile. He could tell them that they would be restored as a people and that other nations would recognize them. The prophet could picture this in the most assuring ways. Not only would they be reestablished as a people, but also they would find a prominent and enviable place among the family of nations.

## How It Happened

The prophet's prediction rang true. Cyrus, the King of Persia, conquered Babylon and became God's instrument for restoring the people of Judah to their homeland. Unfortunately, the rebuilding of the people of God as a formidable nation among others took considerable urging at the behest of later prophets. Also Israel never regained the prestige and respect the nation had once known under David. However, the hopes and dreams of the people of God for a messianic age, when a Second David would come, New Testament writers saw fulfilled in the birth of Jesus of Bethlehem. One can appreciate then why the church has chosen to take the word from the Prophet Isaiah to complement the story of the Magi. The poetic imagery employed by the prophet is to suggest that not only would the people be restored and comforted, but also that the creation itself would be nourished by this event. Then, of course, "the wealth of the Nations" shall also be brought to acknowledge what God had done for God's people. That was to be symbolized by the presence of young camels from Midian and Ephah and the presence of gold and frankincense.

We recognize all of that language as testimony that God has fulfilled in the life of the Infant Jesus what God had done earlier in the history of the people of Israel. We affirm this in what God was able to accomplish in the life, death, and resurrection of our Lord

Jesus Christ. We affirm also that God continues to live and move in history to accomplish the same for those who would recognize that God continues to shine the light of his grace in their lives no matter what comes to threaten, intimidate, or destroy them. As the prophet had to awaken his people to what God was doing for them, so we must continue to witness to the presence of the compassionate God who seeks to deliver us from the darkness of this world.

**The Captivity Of The Church**

The Feast of the Epiphany of our Lord is an important tie for us to remember that as the people of God today we should recognize how easily and how readily we can live in the darkness of this world rather than in the light of God's grace in Christ. We recall how Dr. Martin Luther wrote in 1520 *The Babylonian Captivity of the Church*. Luther found it necessary to address the Church of his day with the fact that the Church was using the sacramental system of the Church itself to keep the people from understanding the freedom that was theirs under the gospel. From age to age the Church has suffered through many different approaches to its own faith that have robbed it of its evangelical character. Pietism in the seventeenth century made its efforts to strengthen the faith of the Church by emphasizing its feelings.

Rationalism in the eighteenth century was a movement to make the faith of the Church perfectly reasonable. Similarly, orthodoxy in the nineteenth the century was the attempt to guarantee the absolute rightness of the faith. Signs of all these movements are ever present temptations of the Church to improve the nature of believing. The difficulty is that each such movement has tended to cast darkness on the purity of the gospel itself. The additions to the gospel, let alone, the subtractions from the gospel, keep us from seeing the light of God's grace as it really is. Those are the problems from within the Church. Then, of course, there are always the threats to the faith from outside the Church. We know that there always will be those who will cast the blanket of darkness on the scene by insisting that the faith is truly folly in the face of the problems that we must face. To celebrate the Epiphany of our Lord is to glory in the fact that God always shines into our hearts to give us the light of faith.

**The Sight**

Walter Cronkite titled his memoirs *A Reporter's Life*. A full life it has been. One can appreciate the fact that his career made him an important witness to so many important events in the latter part of the last century. However, one of his associates, Dick Savant hated Cronkite's signature line, "And that's the way it is" on such and such a date. Mr. Savant argued that the line implied an accuracy of which the reporter was not capable. Mr. Savant was very insightful on that point. Yet when Mr. Cronkite retired, one missed the accuracy of which he was capable. Mr. Cronkite missed it too. A stickler for accuracy, Mr. Cronkite did the very best he could to maintain a standard of integrity and honesty in reporting. Mr. Cronkite became very critical of what happened to the media in general. The growth of the media made them highly competitive, and Mr. Cronkite dubbed their new kind of reporting as "infotainment." The emphasis is more on winning an audience than on reporting the news as it is. Mr. Cronkite's concern was, and ours should be, that we be an informed people who know how it really is. That is very important to people who are free and want to remain free.

As Christians who live in the light of the gospel which God has shined in our hearts that should be even more so. It is not simply in the hearing of the news accurately that we come to understand "the way it is." It is in the light of God's revelation that we come to understand how we are to interpret how things really are. By God"s grace through faith we can interpret what is under the judgment of God and what is under grace. We can identify sin for what it is, and we can identify what is faithful and what is not. That is the call of the Prophet Isaiah on this Epiphany. By faith we are to know that, however it is personally for us this day, we are to rise and shine for our light has come and the glory of the Lord has risen on us.

*Epiphany 1*
*(Baptism Of Our Lord)*

# The Promise Of Baptism

*Isaiah 43:1-7*

---

**William F.** Buckley, Jr., has earned the respect of some of his harshest critics with the publication of *Nearer, My God*. Many of his critics have been among the theologians who have had great difficulty with his rightist opinions. It is not that conservative viewpoints are not welcome, but Mr. Buckley has a penchant for delivering his thoughts in a cavalier style that betrays a snide manner of talking down to people. However, his book *Nearer, My God* is not offensive in its approach to Mr. Buckley's confession of faith. A baptized and confirmed Roman Catholic from his youth, the author reveals a studied approach to the faith that reveals his struggles with the great questions that can trouble us all. Obviously quite satisfied with the strength that he gains from his faith, Mr. Buckley has refrained from making a public display of religious language in the public debates he enjoys immensely.

When Buckley was asked by his publisher to write about his faith, his publisher suggested the title, "Why I am Still a Catholic." Buckley flinched at that, because that suggests there is something wrong with being a Catholic. Likewise, he balked at the title, "Why I am a Catholic." He wanted to express his faith as he understood it. While he does defend the authoritarian approach of the papacy, he also leaves room for critical observations of the practices of his denomination. When one reads the kind of personal confession we get from Mr. Buckley, we are reminded that all of us should be ready to give an autobiography of the faith that is in us. If we were to do so, there would be no better way than for us to begin where our spiritual journey began, namely, in holy baptism. On this First

Sunday after the Epiphany of our Lord, we are helped to understand what happened on that important day in our lives, and why our faith should be so important to us.

## The Baptism Of Israel

The Holy Gospel appointed for today records the Baptism of our Lord. We observe this day as the Baptism of our Lord. It is fitting that the selection from the Hebrew Scriptures as the First Lesson would treat the story of the Israelites as a ritualistic baptism, "When you pass through the waters, I will be with you; and through the rivers, they shall not overwhelm you." The prophet who writes these words is the Second Isaiah. The First Isaiah had conducted his ministry prior to the exile of Judah into Babylon. A second prophet named Isaiah found his calling in assuring the Hebrew exiles that they would return to the land they once had called their own. Working against the blindness and indifference to what God had done for the Hebrews and what God could do again, the prophet does his utmost to rouse the people to an awareness of how God rules in history. The God who had created all and redeemed a special people could recreate them in fulfillment of the promises God had made.

The God of Creation is also the Lord of History. God could use Cyrus, the King of Persia, to bring about the fall of Babylon in the same way that God had caused the Hebrews to fall into the hands of the Babylonians. As a servant of God, Cyrus would permit God's people to return to their homeland in Palestine with protection and every effort to afford complete restoration of this people. As the exiles made their homeward way as they passed through the waters en route, they could think of their traversing those waters as a baptism. The waters that can be so troublesome, so threatening and overwhelming should behave under the rule of the Creator. Instead of drowning and destroying this people, the waters would not behave as the enemy, but, under God's control, the waters would be the assurance of their salvation. The waters, so prominent in God's creation, so necessary for the sustenance of life, so essential to the cleansing and purifying of life, would now perform their best function on behalf of the people. The waters would testify that God was present with them. God says, "When you pass through the waters, I will be with you." The waters would not be ordinary waters, but they would be, by the presence of God, a washing of regeneration and renewal, as the Apostle Paul speaks about the waters of holy baptism. The waters would be the visible witness that God was redeeming and saving this people.

## The Precondition For Baptism

The beauty of this prophetic text is that the prophet explains that God makes it clear that the precondition of the salvation God would prepare in the waters of baptism is what God has done to make the baptism a valid one. The prophet reports that the God who had created, formed, and redeemed this people is the one who says, "Do not fear for I have redeemed you; I have called you by name; you are mine." There are many within Christendom who make the validity of baptism totally dependent upon what the candidate for baptism believes or does. The candidate must make himself or herself worthy of the rite that admits one into the kingdom. In that event, baptism becomes a hoop through which the candidate must jump. Here the prophet recognizes that the waters through which Israel must pass become salvatory, because of what God has already done before the Children of Israel come to the waters. God had created them. God had also recreated them as God's people, that is, God had given them a special and unique call to be the people of God through whom God could reveal God to the world. This redemptive work of God is so unique and so sure that God can say that God has called them by name.

Saying that God was calling Israel by name means more than that their name was to distinguish them from other peoples or nations. In the ancient world a name did more than hang a tag on someone. The name was to represent the nature of the person designated. All of the references to the name of God are to convey the fact that God is totally trustworthy, true, faithful, reliable, just, and good. So it is that the prophet notes that when God says, "I have called you by name," God also says, "You are mine." For the people of God to be called by name means that they belong to God. They are ruled by God, and, as we shall hear, they are called by God's name. So we are not to think of baptism as a name-giving ceremony in the ordinary sense, but in the conviction that in baptism we are granted the very name of God, because we are God's.

## Baptism Is Conditioning

In the case of Israel, the prophet wanted them to understand that in the baptism Israel would have in passing through the waters with the presence of God, God was conditioning them for whatever they had to face. The time of their exile in Babylon would soon be history. The Israelites had to know that the God who had sent them into exile to give them a wake-up call at the hand of Nebuchadnezzar, the Babylonian King, was also the God who would deliver them by the hand of Cyrus, the king of Persia. The experience of God's saving love and grace for them was conditioning them to be able to face whatever trauma would come along the way. The troubled waters would be the sign of their baptism into God's love and grace. So also they could pass through any fiery trials and accept them as a refining process for their betterment. Instead of being consumed by the fires, they could accept them as a maturing process for the children of God. The baptism into the Presence of God should prepare them for all of life.

Our Christian baptism is to do the same for us. When our Lord Jesus Christ was baptized in the River Jordan by John the Baptist, he could well have thought of this beautiful passage from Isaiah. At his baptism God was preparing the beloved Son for the ministry which he was to begin which would be filled with troubled waters and fiery temptations and trials. When Jesus heard the words. "You are my Son, the Beloved," that echoed the word of God from Isaiah, "I have called you by name, you are mine." In the same way our baptism is to remind us that God has conditioned us for life through this act by which he has permitted the waters to be the sign of washing, cleansing, and renewing us for life in all its forms and conditions. We are prepared to face what we must, because we know that the divine resources of God are at our disposal. God is not only in our corner, but God acts on our behalf.

## Baptism Is The Sign Of God's Action On Our Behalf

As the people of Israel would return from exile through the waters of baptism, they could be sure that God would control history for their sake. God says, "I give people in return for you, nations in exchange for your life." The prophet lists the nations that were conquered by the Persians so that Israel could be free. Egypt, Ethiopia, and Sheba would be among them. God also promises that nations to the east or west, north or south would have to relinquish Israelites so that they could be returned to their home. We can only imagine how much the Hebrew people have had to rely on these promises as they have endured exile and persecution one after the other until the worst Holocaust of them all under the Nazis. Yet the Hebrew people endure, because of the promise of God.

As the Hebrew people benefitted from the promise of God in their baptism, so our baptism is a reminder for us that God is always working on our behalf to break the will and purpose of all those who would hinder God's best intentions for us. God gave the Son, the Beloved, in exchange for our lives. In baptism God exchanged our unrighteousness for the righteousness of Jesus Christ. In baptism God exchanged the faithfulness of Jesus for our unfaithfulness. Martin Luther stated over and over again that we should rely heavily on God's promise in Holy Baptism. We can wear our baptism daily. When we are attacked by trials and temptations, we can always throw it in the teeth of the devil that we are baptized. We are not immune to the trials and temptations, but we are assured of victory over them because of God's action on our behalf.

## Baptism Wards Off Fear

Because baptism is an assurance for us that God is always acting on our behalf, our baptism is also reason for us to be confident and trusting. We do not have to fear. Baptism wards off fear. Twice the prophet mentions that we do not have to fear. "Do not fear, for I have redeemed you," God says. And again, "Do not fear, for I am with you." God's attitude toward us is all love. God acts on our behalf, God says, "Because you are precious in my sight, and honored, and I love you." We can be sure that God will not renege on all that is contained in the baptismal covenant of God's grace for us. What it takes is faith and trust that God is serious about the business of loving and caring for us.

In a collection of essays called *Common Ground* three rabbis comment on the Rainbow after the Flood, which God calls a covenant between God and God's creatures and the creation. It was to be a reminder that God would never again destroy the earth as God had done so extensively in the flood. The problem was posed that it is extremely baffling that God should need a reminder. What was even more baffling is that the reminder is somewhat dependent upon being seen by humans. Yet that is how it is. One rabbi noted that the rainbow is significant simply because it is God who created it. Beyond that it is for us that it is created. Consequently it is for us to believe it. So our baptism is a sign for us between God and us in the same way. We can appeal to it always as a reminder that God gave baptism as the sign, and we can trust it, because God stands behind it.

**Baptism Is For The Future**

The crowning feature of the baptism God has created for us is that it is designed for the future. The purpose of Isaiah's word for his people was to assure them that God would deliver them from the exile, but in so doing God was preparing and creating them for the future. They were to share in God's glory. They are the people, God says, "whom I created for my glory." That is the kind of promise God makes in holy baptism. In baptism God promises to raise us from the dead and allow us to enter glory with God. That is what happened to the Beloved Son, Jesus. As Jesus was baptized God gave assurance that God would be with Jesus. And God was. Jesus died on the cross, because people rejected and did not believe God's love, but God raised the Son from the dead. God will do the same for us. That is the baptismal promise. Paul puts it, "We have been buried with him by baptism into death, so that, just as Christ was raised from the dead by the glory of the Father, so we too might walk in newness of life. For if we have been united with him in a death like his, we will certainly be united with him in a resurrection like his" (Romans 6:4-5). Paul's emphasis in this section was on the fact that in baptism we discover new life. Daily we live as the newborn children of God who are privileged to live in the Spirit of God.

In John Updike's novel *Toward the End of Time*, Ben Turnbull is the central character. The story is set in Eastern America in the second decade of the new millennium after a Sino-American nuclear war that had reduced the world's population fifty percent. A retired stock broker, at age 66, Ben finds himself tinkering with other worlds and other times. As a typical Updike character, he represents humanity's entrapment with the mystery of sex. He reminisces. He finds himself caught up in other worlds of other times. He struggles against his own mortality. The struggle with our inevitable mortality is what the novel teaches us. However, as we contemplate our baptism, our future is certain as we move "toward the end of time." By baptism our future is already guaranteed, because we trust that in baptism God has created us for divine glory. We can write our autobiography of faith, because we know the ending. We are destined for glory by baptism to share glory with our Lord Jesus Christ.

*Epiphany 2*

# Light For Beauty

*Isaiah 62:1-5*

---

**David Donald's** biography of Abraham Lincoln is a special effort to help us feel along with Mr. Lincoln the thoughts of his heart and mind as he aspired to the presidency. Mr. Lincoln had an earnest desire to be of special service to the nation he knew was in deep trouble. One senses the compassion he had for all the people. He also recognized that the people could survive only as one nation. No one knew better than he that not everyone would agree with his purpose and will in leading the people. He also knew the terrible price that would have to be paid by people of both the North and the South. He was convinced that the whole matter rested in the hands of God, and prayed God's will would be done in the matter. In due time, Lincoln felt the compelling need to be on the fields with the northern troops to consult with and advise his generals. He wanted to be sure that no one created impediments to achieving peace with mercy and effecting reconciliation between the northern and southern states.

Reconciliation was uppermost in Lincoln's intentions. The reason for ending the war was to restore unity and return to the wholeness that had inspired the creation of the United States. Mr. Lincoln was deeply aware of how differently people in both the North and the South felt about the matter of reconciliation. Mr. Long does not add postlude to his insightful observations of the presidency of Mr. Lincoln. He closes his account with the assassination of Lincoln, which occurred after Lincoln's all too brief enjoyment of the peace. However, it is certain that his death prevented harsher settlements of the peace which would have been more difficult for him to prevent had he lived. In testing these inner thoughts of Lincoln in restoring our nation, one sees parallels in the manner in which the Prophet Isaiah wrote about God's reconciliation with Israel. In the First Lesson appointed for today the prophet describes what was involved in the reconciliation with Israel.

## The Context

In this Epiphanytide we have taken note of the fact that the Church has included readings from the Prophet Isaiah to illustrate how profusely the prophet wrote about God's revelation of the divine will as an epiphany of light. At first, before the Babylonian exile, the Prophet Isaiah could reveal how God would remain faithful to the people in redeeming them in spite of apostasy that precipitated the exile. However, at the close of the exile a Second Prophet Isaiah could herald the good news to these people that God was going to restore this people and return them to their homeland. It is that message about restoration that is the subject of the reading we have before us today. What the prophet wrestled with is how the people could understand the nature of their reconciliation with God. This was no easy task. A nation destroyed, taken into exile, and disgraced as being a nation no more would find it difficult to think of the possibility of being restored as a people.

One does not have to be very old to recognize how often the maps of Europe, Asia, and Africa are changed by military and political conflict. Those of us who are older can speak of change to the names on the face of the globe even more. However, for Israel the disgrace of losing homeland territory was far more devastating. They believed the possession of the land to be part and parcel of the covenant God had made with them beginning with the patriarchs. That they had no land presented particular pain for them, because it meant they no longer were on good terms with Yahweh, their God who had promised that the land God gave them was a sign of the good will with which God had laced the covenant with them.

## No Longer Forsaken

As the prophet makes the effort to stir the people to faith again he writes, "You shall no more be termed Forsaken, and your land shall no more be termed Desolate." People who can remember the late 1960s and early 1970s in America can identify with the feelings of desolation and forsakenness as a pall appeared to fall over us as a people. The civil rights movement had seared the social conscience of the nation, flower children had called into question time-honored institutions throughout the nation, the war in Vietnam had gobbled up economic and human resources over an eighteen-year stretch. The common word was that America had had it. The nation doubted itself, its purpose, and aims. The enterprise of democracy was failing. If you can recall those days or you read about them, you have some sensitivity to what Israel had experienced in exile. Their plight exaggerates the pain that comes to any nation that has undergone the trauma of losing its identity.

What the prophet was saying to the Israelites is that they did not have to languish any longer in their self-doubt and their feelings of desolation and forsakenness. In his book about the collapse of Russian communism, *Down with Big Brother*, Michael Boggs tells about the success of Ronald Reagan. When Robert McFarlaine, one of Reagan's foreign affairs advisers, resigned, he said of Reagan, "He knows so little but he gets so much done." Mr. Reagan's success was attributable to the fact that he believed so firmly in America. He made Americans feel good again about being American. That was the prophet's task. To make the people feel good again about being God's people. It was not how much they knew or could do, but they were to have an implicit faith in the fact that God would restore them.

**Vindicated**

The restoration which God afforded the people of Israel, however, was more than a bold form of nationalism. This restoration was to produce more than a flag-waving kind of patriotism. This restoration was to be a vindication. The prophet says, "The nations shall see your vindication." The vindication did not consist in a declaration of their innocence for not having erred or sinned. Rather the vindication was to be a holy absolution for the manner in which they had dishonored God, but at the same time their God had not given up on them. In that sense their faith was vindicated or defended.

Scott Turow's novel *The Laws of our Fathers* is a helpful account of how we perceive ourselves as a nation. The characters of this story were initially drawn together by the events of the chaotic '60s. They were caught up in the protests of that era on an explosive campus of a California university. The culture was coming apart at the seams. The peace of the Eisenhower years was disrupted by organized life of all forms. Mr. Turow's characters who questioned democracy in the 1960s found themselves united by a criminal law case that raised democratic issues anew for them. Now they found themselves on the other side of the issues. All of us have been affected by what happened in the '60s. Some will say Woodstock won out, and America can never be the same. We have seen the erosion of the really important values and traditions of our society. Others will strongly argue that our American system has been vindicated once again. We survived the '60s. We may modify our lifestyles, but as a people we affirm our democratic ways. If you can understand that argument, you can appreciate how the prophet was trying to awaken the people to what God was doing for them. Israel could be sure they were vindicated by their continuing faith in God. As God's people we know also that in spite of the challenges to our faith, our faith is always vindicated.

**A Special Delight**

What the prophet was trying to instill in the people of Israel was an awareness of the possibilities that were in store for them as the people of God. Returning from the exile in Babylon they should think of themselves as being totally renewed. God would give them a new name to go along with the new status they should enjoy as this redeemed people. They should no longer think of themselves as the forsaken people of God, the desolate people of God, or a people forsaken by God. That was all behind them now. That was in the past. Their future was assured as the people whom God had chosen and rescued once more. The old names of "Forsaken and Desolate" would give way to the new name given by God, "My Delight is in Her." As you have undoubtedly heard many times before, the Hebrew noun not only describes or names something, but it is lively and active. When God calls Israel his delight, that suggests to us that God is actively acting on behalf of Israel in a special way. That is how God thinks about us as the people of God.

When we think we have reason to feel abandoned by God or forsaken by God we can stop being concerned. God has given us every reason to think about ourselves as people in whom God takes special interest and delight. That is what this Epiphany Season is all about. The Epiphany texts are selected to help us see how God reveals himself with special concern in the Person of Jesus. Everything that God did to restore ancient Israel in reclaiming them is the same way God continues to reach out to us. Epiphany is a good time for us to review how God makes special efforts to unfold in fresh and unique ways the nature of God's love and mercy and love for us. The basic conditions are always the same, because people are always the same.

### A Marriage

The language that the prophet employs to describe the earnest effort God makes to impress us with the assurance of love is consistent with the language of apostles and evangelists. Christians are guilty of thinking of themselves as being in a better position than ancient Israel, or they think God behaves better today than in ancient Israel. We do have the advantage of a longer history or having the message packaged better today. However, human nature is just as flawed now as then, and people are as spiritually stupid and indifferent as then. God worked just as hard then as now. The prophet demonstrates that by using an analogy that Jesus used frequently during his ministry. Jesus referred to himself often as a bridegroom coming to take his followers as his bride. The prophet uses the same kind of language. God calls Israel "Married." The prophet goes on, "For as a young man marries a young woman, so shall your builder marry you, and as the bridegroom rejoices over the bride, so shall your God rejoice over you."

We know how the Apostle Paul picked up on marriage as an analogy to describe in a beautiful way the relationship of our Lord

Jesus Christ with the Church. Martin Luther picked up on that analogy and compared it to the rich and influential man who woos the poor and destitute lady to make her his bride. In doing so he confers upon the poor darling all of his wealth and all the assets of his holdings. In doing so he becomes not only her lover but her shield and protection. She is blessed in that she can claim all the holdings and blessings of her husband as her own. Just so in this Epiphanytide we are reminded that our dear Lord Jesus Christ came into the world to reveal that love for us whereby we are married to him and by faith to be advantaged in that he makes his kingdom our own. For us the blessing is not only that we gain in this relationship, but the prophet makes it clear that the delight and joy is just as much for God as it is for us.

## For Or Against The Marriage?

Edward Koch, former mayor of New York City, confesses to a nostalgia and lingering love for the office he held for a number of terms. To nurse his continuing affection for the job, he wrote a novel, *Murder in City Hall*. He spins a mystery tale about his willingness to perform a marriage ceremony for the daughter of a friend. He does this against his better judgment because of the political implications and usual criticisms of favoritism. True to his fears one guest who appears is loathed by all the other guests. Because everyone loathes the unpopular guest, all are held as suspects when the man is killed during the ceremony. The novel revives memories of times when we have been invited to a wedding we did not appreciate. Often we do ask, "Do we have to go?" We might ask the question because someone will be there we do not care to see. We may not have murder in mind, but we might just prefer not having to see certain people. Or it could be that the wedding date falls on a date we have a ticket to an NBA game, the symphony, or a repertoire theater.

The invitation the prophet places before his people is the invitation to their own wedding, the opportunity to permit our relationship with God to enjoy the same intimacy as the relationship of a young couple who are united in marriage. The same holds true for us. In our Lord Jesus Christ, God has given us every reason to believe that we can be on the same intimate terms with God as honeymooners discovering the depth of their relationship of love. Tragically, many good people who want to establish some kind of relationship with God never understand that God has already taken the initiative to make our relationship with him intimate and secure. The promise of God is absolutely sure and true.

## Like A Burning Torch

The prophet uses the most heightened language he can in order to impress upon his people in their exile how attractive God's offer of restoration should be for them. He began this section by writing that God calls out, "For Zion's sake I will not keep silent, and for Jerusalem's sake I will not rest, until her vindication shines out like the dawn, and her salvation like a burning torch." In other words, the prophet envisions that when his people return to their hometown, Zion or Jerusalem, everyone will know about it. This remarkable event will be the return of an exiled people to their home under no duress or force. The return should be the obvious and concrete evidence that God had redeemed and vindicated God's people. The people themselves should radiate this in the very manner in which they return. The joy and peace of that moment should be as bright and glorious as the dawn. The people's sense of being saved would be "like a burning torch."

The people did return as promised, but they did not seem to be as aglow as the prophet had hoped. We can understand that. There are times when no one would have the slightest clue that we enjoy the privilege of being the people nearest and dearest to God's heart. Epiphany is designed to help us understand that God has rescued us from the guilt and shame of being nobodies who have deserved to be outcasts from God's attention. Instead, our Lord Jesus Christ had to die and be risen from the dead for us so that God's love might be revealed in us. We are to be epiphanies of God's love by the way in which we radiate our awareness of God's special love for us. God's love is meant to shine in us like the dawn, and the salvation which is ours by faith should be like a burning torch.

God wants the revelation of his love and mercy to continue in the world. That can only happen when the people who are God's delight and joy can reveal it.

*Epiphany 3*

# Light From The Word

*Nehemiah 8:1-3, 5-6, 8-10*

---

**In the Sundays** of the Epiphany we are reminded in our worship how God continually reveals God's Person. That, of course, is done most clearly in the Person of our Lord Jesus Christ, who came to be one of us. Today the emphasis of the Lessons is on how God is revealed in the Word. In the Holy Gospel, Jesus himself points out how he is revealed in the word, or the word is revealed in him, but the people do not seem to understand. That is always a problem in communication. The words can be ever so clear, but do people get the message? Jeff Shesol deals with this problem in his book *Mutual Contempt*, a study of the tensions between President Lyndon Johnson and the Attorney General Robert Kennedy. The problems began with Kennedy's questioning the advisability of bringing Johnson along as a vice-presidential candidate with his brother Jack as presidential candidate. The jockeying for position and efforts to find common ground led Robert Kennedy to believe that Johnson was an inveterate liar. Johnson and his followers, on the other hand, thought of Johnson as a mediator and an excellent negotiator.

Robert continued to grow in his antagonism toward Johnson for many reasons. When Johnson did serve as Vice President, President Kennedy did ask him to chair a committee dealing with civil rights. At the time Mr. Johnson's committee had no legislation to back them up, but did rely on companies which held government contracts to follow guidelines for the hiring of African-Americans. Both Robert and Jack Kennedy showed impatience that not more was being done. The Vice President kept pointing to the fact that no law was in place for them to enforce a policy for hiring. The problem was always whether people believed the word or not. The problem continues to this day. Since then there has been considerable legislation to protect civil rights. Yet the problem is whether the legislation is enforced or not. It is one thing to communicate the intent of the word of the law, but the problem is whether people understand, observe, or obey or not. That is what today's Lessons are about. The First Lesson from the book of Nehemiah relates what Ezra and Nehemiah did about bringing the matter of the word of God to the attention of the people.

**The Context**

The Lesson is taken from the book of Nehemiah. The books of Ezra and Nehemiah are accounts of the return of Jewish exiles to Jerusalem from Babylonia. Originally the books were known as 1 and 2 Ezra, based on the memoirs and the records of both Ezra and Nehemiah. There has been some effort to prove that Ezra was the author of both books. However, it is more likely that neither Ezra nor Nehemiah were the author of either book. There is no evidence that Ezra and Nehemiah ever met in their roles as leading the returned exiles to rebuild the holy city of Jerusalem. Nehemiah is a layman and a eunuch who had served as cupbearer in the court of Artaxerxes at Susa. Ezra is a scribe who develops a strong leadership role for his people. Each of the men were involved in leading groups of their people from Babylon to Jerusalem.

The return of the exiles occurred in stages over a long period of time lasting some one hundred years. The first return of exiles was in 538 B.C. under Cyrus. There was an attempt to rebuild the Temple, but it was not completed because of opposition. The Temple was rebuilt with encouragement from the prophets Haggai and Zechariah at the time of the second return of exiles about the year 520 B.C. In the next generation it was Ezra who led some of the exiles back to the holy city. Then, probably a whole generation later, Nehemiah led exiles back to their homeland. The task for the leaders who brought back the people was not only to inspire them to return but then also to give them encouragement to get the people to organize themselves, rebuild the city, and establish themselves as the people of God once more. What we have before us today in the First Lesson is an account of how Ezra organized the people to share with them the word of God for the formation of their lives together.

**The Task**

What we have is the record of how the people met together for the reading of the word from God. We are not sure how the books of Ezra were originally organized chronologically, so even though this text is found in what appears to be the memoirs of Nehemiah, the story's central character is Ezra. We read that it was in the beginning of the month of Tishri when this took place, for them possibly the beginning of a new year, an ideal time to begin anew. That would be late September or early October on our calendar. It was the people who organized themselves and requested that Ezra come and read "the book of the law of Moses, which the Lord had given to Israel." We cannot be sure of how much of the "book of the law of Moses" was meant. We know that it was not in book form as we see things printed out, but the book was a scroll that had to be unrolled in order to make the point. How much scroll had to be read is debatable. The term "law" in the Hebrew Scriptures normally is generic for the whole of God's revelations. Or it could be that only Deuteronomy was read. It has also been suggested that portions of the Scriptures were read with interpretations or additions that fit the situation in which the Jerusalem population found itself.

As it was, the people of Jerusalem found themselves at a crucial moment in their history. It must have been at least 800 years since their forefathers, released from bondage in Egypt, had received the covenant from God through the Mediator Moses at Mount Sinai. For forty years their ancestors were providently cared for in the wilderness and moved into the Promised Land of Canaan. They occupied, conquered, and settled that land and eventually created a glorious monarchy that thrived under the administration of an outstanding king by the name of David. Tragically the kingdom involved itself in civil war that divided the kingdom into the Northern Kingdom of Israel and the Southern Kingdom of Judah. In time the infidelity and idolatries in the Northern Kingdom led to its downfall in 722 B.C. The Assyrians ravaged the nation and carried the ten tribes of the North into captivity and scattered them to the four corners of the earth never to return. Judah, the Southern Kingdom, suffered defeat and exile to Babylonia in 586 B.C. Now in this slow recovery of the population through four different returning groups, the people of Jerusalem had to regroup and decide about their future.

**The Word**

The people gathered in the city square early in the morning to hear the priest Ezra read the word to them. They remained until noon, which means that the reading took about six hours. The situation was reminiscent of when Moses read the Law to the people before they entered into the Promised Land. That we know as Deuteronomy, which means the Second Giving of the Law. Ezra's reading was a repetition once more of giving of the Law as a way for God to make a claim on this people. The Hebrew understanding of a reading of the Law as the word of God was that one should relate to it as though it were being read for the first time. That is to say, the reading of the word would have the same effect or power as though God were revealing it in its initial or pristine form. This was not second hand stuff. The word Ezra was reading to the people was as lively, active, and effective as the word Moses had read to the people eight hundred years before and as King Josiah had the law read to the people in his efforts to instill spiritual reforms in his day.

It is important for us to have the same kind of understanding of the use of the word in our day. Ezra knew that the assemblage of the people of Jerusalem around the word of God was essential if they were to define themselves as the people of God once more. The people could attempt all kinds of social reforms and struggle with the actual rebuilding of their city in vain if they did not acknowledge their history and tradition as the people of God. That, too, would be in vain if they did not live under the same covenant, the same promises, and the same rule of God which had shaped the history of their forbears. Here was the moment in which they could experience God's presence in and among them. They would be confronted in the same manner as we hear in the Holy Gospel that the people of Nazareth were confronted by Jesus. When Jesus read the word of God to them from the Prophet Isaiah, Jesus said to them, "Today the Scripture has been fulfilled in your hearing." For the people in the synagogue in Nazareth this was a dramatic modeling of what is always going on in the word. God is always present in the word to confront us.

**The Reaction**
The reaction of the people is that there was mourning and weeping. Before we ask ourselves what this public lamenting meant, we should take note of the fact that this assemblage was constituted of both men and women. What is noteworthy of that is not that the scene was the more emotional because of the presence of women. The Hebrew Scriptures do not reserve emotional reactions to women. Weeping is as much a male trait as it is a female trait. What is important to recognize is that normally it was not required of the women to take part in the religious ceremonies. That was a must only for the men. Here both the people and Ezra apparently want to make a new start at things and involve everyone. The intention was that these people did not want to let happen to them what had taken place in the lives of their ancestors to bring on them the shame and pain of the exile. No doubt their weeping and their mourning at the reading of the word was to recognize that the exile could have been avoided if only the people had trusted the word of the Lord who had covenanted with them.

The reaction of tears and mourning must have been a mixed reaction of the people. On the one hand, there must have been a great deal of guilt that was followed by a genuine sense of repentance for the previous indifference to the word of God. On the other hand, there had to be great deal of joy when the people also learned that God was a gracious and forgiving God who had not only not given up on them but who still wanted them as God's own. All of that had to be tempered by a grim determination of the people not to repeat the sordid history of the unbelief, the indifference to the word, and the outright idolatry. The people did affirm what they heard of the word of God. They responded with the spontaneous but liturgical amens, which meant that they were in agreement with what they heard. They lifted their hands as a sign of agreement with what they heard from on high. What was most important, "Then they bowed their heads and worshiped the Lord with their faces to the ground." These acts of worship would indicate more than contrition, but also adoration of God that was prompted by their humility and faith before him.

**The Feast**

Ezra himself must have been moved by the reaction of the people. He was touched by the fact that they were prompted to tears and that they did respond in an affirmative manner. In turn, Ezra announced to the people, "This day is holy to the Lord your God; do not mourn or weep." By this Ezra indicated to the people that their affirmation of what had been read to them was the kind of response God was looking for. God accepted their confession as making the covenant between God and people secure and effective for them. They did not have to mourn or weep but rather they could get about the business of making the covenant alive and real in their lives. In other words, Ezra was pleased that he could see good results to the effort that had been made to have the people understand the kind of mutual claim that God and people had on one another. Interpreters cite this occasion as the beginning of Judaism. This was the start of recognizing that the unique role the people of the former Southern Kingdom would have to play in the family of nations was to behave and define themselves as the people of God, the chosen ones.

Ezra also added that the people could celebrate what had transpired between them and God. He urged them, "Go your way, eat the fat, and drink sweet wine, and send portions to those for whom nothing is prepared, for this day is holy to your Lord; and do not be grieved, for the joy of the Lord is your strength." The people could celebrate the goodness of the Lord. Typically a feast is the occasion in which we not only taste of the good things before us, but also we discover a deepening of our sense of community. We all know those times when we have felt spent in giving strict attention to a learning experience of a lecture, seminar or special meeting. Then the meal afterwards becomes more than an occasion for relaxation and refreshment. The meal becomes a communion, the meeting of hearts, minds, and spirit, as people share together in the fraternity of a meal.

**A Call For Faith**

It is very important for us to catch the flavor of what Ezra was doing for the people on this important occasion. There are many interpreters who fault Ezra for the creation of Judaism as a provincial, exclusive, and legalistic version of the Hebrew faith. They point to his ruling that the Jews should not marry outside the faith as typical of this narrow view of the faith. That would be unfair to the larger task which Ezra performed, which was to get the people to return to the faith as well as to interpret and to practice the faith. Our story mentions over and over again that all this was done with interpretation and that the Levites were given the assignment of helping the people to understand all that was involved. Ezra saw his task as beginning back on square one to get people to appreciate the special place they had in the heart and the mind of God.

We in America should have a sympathetic understanding of what Ezra was trying to do. We have all kinds of people stressing the fact that we as a people need to recapture what it means to be American. Educators, politicians, pastors, professionals, talk show hosts and hostesses, and business men regularly talk about recapturing values and of redeveloping the cultural awareness that made our nation great. That often means going back into our history to examine what a makes frontier nation great. As Christians we should always be about that task. As Ezra called the people back to the covenant, we need to rehearse the gospel of salvation over and over again in our worship, be given to the study of God's word so that we can apply it, and be regularly in communion with one another at the Lord's feast. Our Lord Jesus Christ not only made that necessary for us by his own exemplary life but also he is the fulfillment of the covenant Ezra shared with the people. Jesus died and rose again, so that the covenant is for real for us by the manner in which he comes to us, which is through the word and sacraments. He is even more. He not only fulfills the word, but he is the interpretation of it. He is the one who gives light through the word.

*Epiphany 4*

# The Light Touch

*Jeremiah 1:4-10*

---

**Robert Bly has** given us a painful and scathing analysis of our present American society. He titled his work *The Sibling Society*. Bly confesses he began this work in a lighthearted vein. He employed poetry, fairy tales, and legends to highlight the contradictions he noted all around him. However, he soon discovered that he was into some really serious business. Essentially, what he uncovered was that we are all swimming in a tank of half-adults. For Bly, Elvis and Woodstock were watersheds at which time all parents lost their children. That is to say, the society in which we live cannot be considered paternalistic or materialistic. Authority, boundaries, limits, and traditions are gone. Adolescence starts earlier and lasts all the way to age 35. Even then we have our ability to mature to the stature that commands respect.

We are all equals, all brothers and sisters, all siblings. We keep slipping back into adolescence. We are confused by what is going on around us, because structure and boundaries are missing. In addition, as we struggle with the foibles of the sibling society, we have mixed feelings. We have difficulty mounting the courage and mettle to deal with many issues that require not only maturity but also commitment, bravery, and firmness of mind to deal with the serious issues that confront us. In the First Lesson appointed for today we hear that kind of confession from Jeremiah who protests a call from God to serve as God's prophet to the people of Judah. Jeremiah struggles against the call from God, arguing that he is still a boy, a youth, a tender lad who could not handle such a high calling.

## The Context

Jeremiah had good reason to think twice about answering the call of God to minister to the people of Judah. Jeremiah was a highly sensitive man. He was emotional and felt deeply for his people. It did not take a ton of bricks to fall on his head for him to take note of the fact that his people were highly vulnerable to attack from other world powers. As now, the Israelites were in a strategic location in the Middle East that made them a crossroad to the sea, the Mediterranean. The situation was somewhat different for them than from the conditions today in the Middle East. Today, Israel is surrounded by smaller powers of Arab nations. However, it is Iraq which seems to be obsessed with the notion that if it were to destroy Israel with atomic weapons, it would be the toast of the rest of the Arab nations. In Jeremiah's day, the threat came to Judah from other nations, but there was always a superpower like Babylonia looking for ways to extend its domination and influence in the world.

Judah should have learned from the Northern Kingdom of Israel what kind of fate awaited a people of its own tradition when they did not heed the word of God. Judah and Israel had suffered great mutual antagonisms, because they were so strongly related both by blood and by the word they had from God. At times they joined forces to ward off common enemies. Yet the Northern Kingdom fell, because the nation had been indifferent to the word of God the prophets witnessed to it. Now the Southern Kingdom of Judah was inviting disaster and judgment because of the same kind of hard-hearted attitudes toward the word of God.

## Jeremiah's Resistance

One can appreciate why Jeremiah would be reluctant to be excited about the call that he received from God to minister to the people of Judah. Jeremiah was not yet twenty years old when he sensed he was being called by God. Someone else may have been flattered by the notion that he was being drawn into God's service at a youthful age. Not Jeremiah. He would have had good reason for feeling at home and comfortable in the work of the Lord, because he had grown up in a rectory, the home of his father Hilkiah, a village priest in Anatoth in the land of the tribe of Benjamin. That meant he came from a long line of priests. However, that did not prompt Jeremiah to give a quick affirmative reply to God's call to the office of prophet.

It was not simply Jeremiah's youth that kept him from responding enthusiastically to the prophetic task. The young man complained that he did not know how to speak. Translated that meant he did not know what he could say under the circumstances. He did not have experience in this field. It was one thing to absorb the practices of the priesthood from his father, grandfather, and uncles. Those tasks were prescribed carefully, and he undoubtedly relished the privilege of the clinical experiences of priestly routines right within his own home. How would he acquire the ability to articulate words that would represent the thoughts of God for his people? In an era of high devotion and loyalty to God that might be easy, but Jeremiah had great misgivings about his people.

**God's Call**

It was typical of the prophetic calling that those who assumed the high calling of representing God to God's people did so with a good measure of reluctance. God drags the candidates for the prophetic roles into divine service in spite of their protests, their yelling and screaming about inadequacies, and their fear for their lives. What God has to say to them, however, far outweighs any objections the ill-prepared candidates can muster to make themselves exempt from service. Even before Jeremiah mounted his protestation, God made a convincing argument as to why Jeremiah was chosen. God had an eye on Jeremiah before Jeremiah was born. This was a pre-natal determination on the part of God, because God foresaw that Jeremiah would be properly prepared by his parents for the task to which God could consecrate him for the nations.

When Jeremiah did try to object to the call of God by relying on the crutch of his youthfulness, God had a ready answer. God indicated that all this talk about boyishness was beside the point, because God was the one who was sending Jeremiah. God would pick the targets for Jeremiah, and God would also make clear what Jeremiah should declare to his audience. The clincher was that God could say, "Do not be afraid of them, for I am with you to deliver you." The prophetic office was God's work. God would choose the mission, God would provide the words, and God would be present to make the work effective. The young boy Jeremiah could take up this calling with supreme confidence.

**God's Touch**

As an affirmation and confirmation of the calling which God laid upon Jeremiah, Jeremiah relates, "Then the Lord put out his hand and touched my mouth." We do not know in what manner or way that this took place. However, we do know that this symbolic action was highly significant. Later God says to Jeremiah, "You shall serve as my mouth" (15:19). We know also that in the call of the Prophet Isaiah (Isaiah 9:6), God does the same thing by touching the prophet with a coal to purify the mouth for the task of sharing the word. The important item for us to understand is that the word is to be shared by word of mouth. The word is to be proclaimed, dialogued, preached, taught, pored over in seminars, and meditated on in groups.

Luther asserted that the word is a *mundhaus*, that is a "mouth house." He found that preferable to a *federhouse*, that is the "feather house." By that he meant that the word is to be shared more by speaking than by writing. The Hebrew rabbis also have said that it would be far more preferable that the word remain in an oral tradition than in a written tradition. The reason for these preferences for the oral word is that the word is to be personally applied and personally witnessed. We all know that to be true. We feel much more efficient in a learning situation when the teacher is present to explain and to give the assignment meaning and life.

**God's Word**

In addition to a personal application of the word, the prophetic task was to be effective, because it was involved with the word of God. God said to the prophet Jeremiah, "Now I have put my words in your mouth." The prophet was Jeremiah. The word was God's. The very title "prophet," means to "speak on behalf of." Jeremiah would speak on behalf of God. The Hebrew name by which the prophets were called is *nabim*. The exact origin of that name is not known, but it came to mean "announcer." The prophet announced what God wanted the people to hear. The term *nabim* also came to connote someone inspired by the Spirit of God. The prophets were regarded as the "insane," that is, "out of their own minds," because they represented the mind of God or the Spirit of God.

The word which the prophet Jeremiah was to share on behalf of God was a lively word, because God would accomplish what the word has to say. Later Jeremiah could say that the word of God is a fire which can devour the people (5:14). Or again the people could understand that the word is a hammer that shatters the most stubborn rock (23:29). What is most important is that God's word is always fulfilled. God accomplishes what God says God will do. God keeps God's word. When God promises anything, it is as good as done. The greatest accomplishment, the most difficult miracle God performs through the word, is to make believers out of people. That is the prophetic task and calling.

**Our Calling**

No doubt, all of us have in one way or another sensed the inadequacy Jeremiah felt when he was called to the prophetic office. We think of the many times we hope that no one will call on us to serve on an evangelism committee or team. Or we may have offered feeble excuses when asked to serve in some capacity in which we would have to speak out about the word or the church. We feel our ineptitude, our lack of experience, and our conviction that we just won't have the right words to say. Most of us do not feel we have the ability to talk about anything publicly, let alone our faith. Nor do we feel that we can sell anything, least of all our faith. It is highly unlikely that God finds those answers acceptable, though they are so very, very true.

What God would expect of us, in whatever opportunity we have to share the word, is to share exactly what Jeremiah was called to share. Jeremiah was not called to share his word, but the word of God, and God gave that to him. Just so, God has given the word to us. We know God's love and grace in the Person of Jesus Christ, who lived, died, and rose again for us. All that we are ever asked to proclaim in speaking on behalf of God is just what that has meant to us and means to us. We know what forgiveness means. We know what it means to be loved by God. And we know that God is perfectly willing to share eternity with us. Those are the words God has put in your heart, and God will also put them on your lips.

**A Superior Calling**

Jeremiah's timidity about speaking on behalf of God faded with God's assurance that God would equip him with the message to speak to others. Likewise we should not really have a problem deciding what we should say. Ben Bradlee, former editor of the *Washington Post,* relates in his autobiography *A Good Life* what difficult choices an editor has to make in deciding what to print. An intimate friend of President Jack Kennedy, Bradlee was reminded by Jacqueline Kennedy that he had to protect the privacy of the White House family. Bradlee's most famous decision was to push on with the exposure of the Watergate fiasco which led to the resignation of President Richard Nixon. Someone told Bradlee that editors are simply writing a rough draft of history. Editorial choices are not easy. That is not our problem when it comes to sharing the news and the word about God.

God has written the script and made the editorial choices for us. Our Lord Jesus Christ himself is the Word of God Incarnate. What Jesus has done for us says it all. Too often our problem is that we think that we must find new, clever, or heady ways to express it. That is the opposite of the timidity that is usually our first excuse. By thinking that we have to have special wordsmiths to do the job we make new excuses for ourselves. We do not have to do that. What we need to do is simply share the experience of being loved and cared for by God. When God was finished getting that point across to Jeremiah, God could say to him that God would appoint him over nations and kingdoms "to pluck up and to pull down." Jeremiah was able to speak not only about the lot of the people Israel, but he could also announce how God ruled in the history of the other nations of his day. We can take heart that the word which we do share as the gospel of our Lord Jesus Christ has that kind of force and power in the lives of people. Jeremiah went on to do the work of God. All of us know we will not match what he achieved. Nor is it likely that we will have to suffer what he did. Yet because, he did what he did, we can take heart that what we do in the name of our God will also take effect.

*Epiphany 5*

# Light
# To Serve

*Isaiah 6:1-8 (9-13)*

---

**One of the** last works which James Michener published was *The Noble Land: My Vision for America*. During his long and distinguished writing career Mr. Michener had researched voluminous materials to describe the rise and fall of many civilizations as the settings for his novels. As Michener wrote about America, his homeland, he did so with thanksgiving and appreciation. Gratefully he acknowledged that America had treated him well. However, he observed that there has been considerable slippage in America's cultural values. In spite of the fact that our American method of governing ourselves is the most enduring form of government in human history, Mr. Michener believed that twilight may set in for this nation about the year 2050. The elderly Michener expressed his wish that he could be here to administer changes that would avoid catastrophe for our culture. As he sensed his approaching death, that, of course, was not possible. As he offered his suggestions for correcting what he knew to be wrong, Mr. Michener was not alone in expressing a pessimistic view of America's future.

As we try to offset negative views of our future, serious students of government would remind us that though we have halted the nuclear arms race, we sit in the shadows of nuclear stockpiles capable of destroying civilization in the blink of an eyelash. We face the awesome responsibility of trying to remove those stockpiles without blowing ourselves to kingdom come. In addition, we have entered the era of terrorism of major dimensions. We also have the environmentalists threatening us with horrendous scenarios of how we endanger our land as well as our planet. If you can appreciate the role of those who try to alert us to the dangers of our future, you can sense what the role of an Old Testament prophet was.

**The Context**

In the First Reading appointed for today we have an account of the calling of the Prophet Isaiah in the Temple at Jerusalem. We know very little about the person of the Prophet Isaiah, the son of Amoz. We do know that he ministered to the people of Judah, the Southern Kingdom, for about a generation from 742 to 701 B.C., or perhaps even up until 687 B.C., when the Southern Kingdom fell. The Northern Kingdom had already fallen and was annexed to the Assyrian empire. Judah lived as a vassal state, with the fate of the Northern Kingdom as a political lesson in the harsh realities that can befall any nation that is weakened from within. It was in this political milieu that Isaiah came on the scene to inform his people of the pessimistic future that awaited them. Isaiah was not singular in this calling. His contemporaries were Amos, Hosea, and Micah. Though our collections of the writings of Isaiah's contemporaries are limited, their voices in Isaiah's day were not. Isaiah's preaching and teaching would be in much the same tradition as his colleagues.

The little we do know about Isaiah is offset by the fact that we can surmise that he is also a priest. We can make that conjecture on the basis of the lesson before us today, which locates his service in the Temple where he has a special spiritual experience of being able to see the presence of God in a remarkable vision. We can also surmise that Isaiah was a priest from the manner in which he expresses himself on occasion. It is of small importance that we do not know more about Isaiah. We think of him as the First Isaiah who forewarned and foretold that destruction was eminent if the people did not repent. This is the first prophet by that name. Later in the exile another prophet using the same name would call the people back to the faith. In order to understand the complexity of the task of the First Isaiah, we do well to study carefully how he was called into service.

## The Reluctance Of Isaiah

Isaiah's call occurring in the Temple would of itself be no guarantee that he was a priest. However, the description of that momentous experience suggests that this happened in the holy of holies. Isaiah had a vision of God sitting upon a throne, like a king in regal attire, attended by seraphim who have extraordinary winged features. The seraphim chanted antiphonally the trisagion, the thrice-holy acclamation about the presence of the God who fills the whole earth with divine glory. The antiphonal voices shook the very timbers of the holy place, and the entire area filled with smoke, one more sign of the presence of the Holy One. The experience was overwhelming for the priest Isaiah. The design of the liturgical worship and the worship place for the Hebrews was that the priest would enter the holy of holies to act and serve on behalf of the people. The purpose of this arrangement was to assure the people that as the priest made a tryst with God, they could know that God was truly present on their behalf.

On this given day, however, Isaiah experienced more than the usual impressive presence of the ark of the covenant which represented the presence of God. Isaiah sensed the presence of God in this unique vision of the reality of God. The priest was petrified by what was happening before him. He exclaimed, "Woe is me! I am lost, for I am a man of unclean lips, and I live among a people, of unclean lips; yet my eyes have seen the King, the Lord of hosts." Isaiah can only utter his shame as a sinner unworthy of the vision before him. The same would be true for the whole lot of people he represented. No one person he knew would be worthy of the experience he just had in viewing the King. The presence of the Holy One revealed his unworthiness and sinfulness. There was no way God would have anything to do with him, or that Isaiah could be of service to God.

## The Unworthiness Of Isaiah

The reluctance of Isaiah to respond to the presence of the King was not a polite gesture on his part. Isaiah was not indulging in the kind of false modesty most of us resort to when we really want to be coaxed into something. Nor was Isaiah merely self-conscious about this radically new experience as he performed his usual stint in the holy of holies. Rather, Isaiah was deeply aware how keenly we should feel the burden of our guilt and shame in the presence of our Creator. All of us should sense the same emotions as Isaiah as we approach our worship. As a place set apart where we can be confronted by the presence of the holy, our worship space suggests that. Our liturgy reminds us of our need to confess before God our unworthiness either to hear the word or to partake of the sacrament of God's presence.

Sometimes our conversations about God, our jokes about God, and our arguments about God betray the fact that we may take the presence of our Holy God rather casually. Some people are extremely flippant about how they should behave in worship. The Old Testament worship which gave shape to the worship of the New Testament people of God was most serious about the manner in which to approach God. All of that was exaggerated for Isaiah as he experienced this dramatic revelation of God. Though he had served as a priest conscientiously, faithfully, and prayerfully, suddenly he was stung with the pain of how sinful he really was. He had the right to speak neither for himself nor for the people whom he served. We are not told whether or not Isaiah sensed immediately that this unique experience of God's presence was to initiate a new calling for Isaiah. We do get the feeling that Isaiah did know that God had something special in store for him, and Isaiah did not feel up to it. Isaiah felt utterly unusable.

**The Redemption Of Isaiah**

In a striking gesture one of the seraphim flew to Isaiah with a live coal that had been taken from the altar of sacrifice. The seraph then touched the mouth of Isaiah with the coal. That sounds rather frightening and hurtful. However the action was meant to be one of cleansing and purifying. That is how the seraph explains it. "Now that this has touched your lips, your guilt has departed and your sin is blotted out." There was no way Isaiah could have cleansed or saved himself, but by this sacramental action God saves and purifies the man Isaiah. We think of how God does the same for us in the sacramental life by which he touches us to blot out our sin and unworthiness. God shares the sacrifice our Lord Jesus Christ made for us by his death and resurrection through sacramental means so that we not only hear but are also touched with the righteousness of Christ.

John Updike relates how people can struggle with their awareness of their inadequacy and unworthiness in his novel *In the Beauty of the Lilies*. The story begins with Clarence Wilmot, a tender soul and highly sensitive Presbyterian pastor, who loses the faith. The reader wrenches through the pain of Wilmot's struggle and what that all means to his family. The story concludes with Esau, Wilmot's great grandson, who catches a glimmer of redemptive faith in the ill-fated fiery conflagration of a zany community of would-be-believers. The story Updike weaves through three generations of the same family emphasizes how the imperfections and flaws dominate their relationship more than any strengths or beauty they might offer to one another. The story begs for the kind of cleansing experienced by the sacramental action of the holy God revealed to him. Updike's story is a good parable on how generation after generation can miss the offer God makes in God's presence.

**The Call**

There was no mistaking the presence of God at this moment. Isaiah was fully aware of the fact that God had taken away any excuse he could make to dodge the impact God had made upon his life. This was a dramatic experience for him. It is the kind of experience we would all like to have to assure us that God is in our lives. However, no angel, with its holy smoke and a passel of angels calling to one another, does appear to duplicate this extraordinary event. For Isaiah there is no escape from this arresting scene and the word that follows. When Isaiah's objection and resistance are overcome, when he has been thoroughly cleansed for the job, he hears the voice of the Lord, "Whom shall I send, and who will go for us?" God does not go to those who neither acknowledge God's presence in their lives nor have not been prepared to be received into the kingdom or rule of God by cleansing and faith.

For us the call may appear to be lackluster, mundane, or too ordinary. Yet, however the call comes, it is a call from God. For

Isaiah the call came when he was at his work, doing what he should have been doing. Normally, that is where we meet God. God calls out to us from what we have in hand. We may be at the computer, at the dishwasher, at the lathe, in the car, or at any other place of vocation. But that is what it is, a vocation, a calling, a place where God calls out to us to do God's bidding. When we see that, or understand that, whatever mundane task we are doing lights up in a new way. In what we are doing we hear God calling out to us to serve our neighbor by doing God's bidding for that task.

**The Answer**

The answer Isaiah gave is not a part of the appointed reading for today. However, we all know that Isaiah responded, "Here am I; send me!" Isaiah sensed that in the very act of the call God also gave the power to respond in the affirmative. God was not asking the impossible. God did not require the prophet to do something God would not furnish either the strength or the word for doing what God would require of him. Isaiah was right about that. God did furnish a word. Immediately God instructed Isaiah, "Go and say to this people the following." Isaiah was never at a loss for words to instruct the people in how to read the signs of the times, how to repent, and what to expect of the judgment, the providence, and the redemption of God. We know how effective the prophet was in delivering his message. He remains the foremost of the prophets not only in the place he occupies in the Scriptures, but in the manner in which we today are able to find his work applicable to our day.

Now it could be that God would once again raise a prophet from among us as God did with Isaiah. However, more than likely the majority of us shall not have such a calling, but God calls us nonetheless. What God requires of us, however, is a calling to live and act in the awareness that God is at our side requiring of us faithfulness in the performance of our duties for the sake of our neighbor. Not all of us have the same opportunities to be vocal about the faith, but we can be demonstrative of the faith in the manner in which we perform our duties. Then again many of us have opportunities to speak for the faith which we hold and confess.

**Jesus Shows How**

The whole matter of our calling is illustrated in the Holy Gospel for today, The Great Draught of Fishes. The story is so well known it does not have to be repeated. However, the story does illustrate that the call of our Lord came to men who were engaged in their vocation, which was fishing. Jesus uses the draught of fishes to teach them that the obedience to his word enables them to have great success at their work. Jesus tells them that he can do the very same thing for them in catching people. For them the lesson was a dramatic illustration how the word of God works. They could see the result in their nets, but they would not always be able to see the results of their work among people in the same way.

We can take heart the same way. What the Season of Epiphany is designed to do is to make us alert to the light God has shined into our lives through the incarnation of our Lord Jesus Christ. The Christ who lived, died, and rose again for us made it possible for us to see life in the light of all that he revealed. Because of that, we are the called people of God to be sent into the world to serve God by whatever means and in whatever circumstances we find ourselves. In the light of all that God has done for us in Christ Jesus, we can all respond to the presence of God by saying, "Here am I; send me!"

*Epiphany 6*

# The Fruit Of One's Doings

*Jeremiah 17:5-10*

---

**A biography of** Humphrey Bogart by Sperber and Lax portrays the star of the golden era of Hollywood as a troubled man. Bogart reached stardom in Hollywood as only a limited number have. He was the leading male box office attraction. He was financially secure. He married Lauren Bacall. Yet his discomfort with what he did was obvious always to those who knew him. He worked intensely at his craft. Yet one day while on the set making a new film, he remarked, "What a way to make a living!" On one occasion a friend noted how crestfallen Bogart was. The friend asked Bogart why he was always so unhappy. Bogart replied that he expected a lot more from himself, and he also knew he would never get it.

The gnawing dissatisfaction that filled the life of Bogart might help to explain his alcoholism and his smoking which combined to take his life at the age of 57. At times Mr. Bogart gave evidence of literary and speaking skills which make one wonder how much he quietly berated himself for failing to make better use of his gifts. All of us know that feeling to some extent. Yet Mr. Bogart represents the kind of case history of how devastated one's life can be if one does not experience a way in which one can deal with the failure to achieve what one ought to be. For that reason it is a wholesome exercise to examine the First Reading appointed for today. In this lesson the Prophet Jeremiah draws a contrast between the lives of those who live dependent upon their own resources alone and those who rely upon God.

**The Context**

People who have only a brushing acquaintance with Jeremiah think of the prophet as being highly vitriolic and extremely harsh on his people. That would be to know the man only for his reputation of speaking judgments upon his people for their failure to trust the covenant of God. In reality, Jeremiah was a deeply sensitive person who suffered much emotional depression about the fate of his people because they did not respond to calls to repentance. Jeremiah knew that his people were sowing the seeds of their own destruction, because they were indifferent to God's promises to embrace and protect them in the face of the enemy. God would rescue them if only they would trust and rely upon God for divine providence rather than to rely upon political treaties, prosperity, and their armed forces. It is no wonder then that we have this considerable collection of oracles from Jeremiah which lash out at the hard-heartedness of Israel.

However, that is not all we have from Jeremiah. He could also assure them that God would in time redeem and save them in spite of their indifference at this moment in their history. Jeremiah also served as a teacher to demonstrate how the relationship with God should be characterized. That is what we have before us today. The chapter from which this psalm is taken begins with a statement bemoaning the plight of Israel in which by their "own act" they would spoil the heritage God had planned for them. Then, using the model of Psalm 1, Jeremiah paraphrases the Psalm to remind the people that they would not have to be a part of any negative response to God's designs. There is no reason why the people of God should be put to shame. They are born by the spirit of God to enjoy the privileges that God is willing to offer them — God's loving providence and care. There definitely is hope for them to be able to cope with whatever trials or temptations come their way.

**The Problem**

The prophet explains that the reason people make it difficult for themselves is that they turn "their hearts away from the Lord" in order to trust in "mere mortals" and "make flesh their strength." Most certainly the prophet would not rule out the fact that we all experience wholesome and loving experiences in people. That would be particularly true of receiving good instruction and upbringing from our parents. Nor would the prophet rule out the role models we have had in growing up and maturing. What would be threatening or disrupting in our lives is if the people who influenced our lives were not believing and trusting themselves. Either such people would be keeping us from being able to trust God or they would be discouraging that trust. Instead they would be making themselves the models of strength and help, and we would be counting on the wrong kind of help; help that would ultimately fail us. That sounds relatively easy. We should be able to discern who are the good people to emulate. Yet it is not always so.

The prophet says that the "heart is devious above all else; it is perverse — who can understand it?" When you get down to cases, behavior is not all that easy to analyze. God says that God has to "test the mind and search the heart" to get at things the way they are. However, that is never easy. People are highly complicated. It is not easy to get at what makes them tick or what controls their thoughts and their ideas. That is especially true of what they believe in. They can have all kinds of reasons for not believing God. God wants them to have good reason to believe in God.

**Be Like The Father**

An art exhibit that has traveled the country is titled "Mary Cassatt: Modern Woman." Mary Cassatt was an American artist who worked principally in the last century in France as an impressionist painter closely associated with Degas. In her middle years and during the last decade of the nineteenth century, Cassatt featured principally mothers and children in her paintings. Having never married herself, she was deeply touched mainly by the bond between mothers and daughters. Her paintings reflect quite plainly the emotional and sensual feelings between mothers and daughters. The subject of children also reflects the commonly held notion of the day that children are innocent. One painting featuring a group admiring one child was believed to have been inspired by one of the nativity scenes of the Holy Child. One striking painting of a parent and child focused on a father and son. The subjects were Cassatt's brother and nephew. The resemblance between father and son arrest the attention of the viewer. The eyes of both father and son penetrate the same way. Their features are most similar, suggesting that the son will grow to be a clone of the father. What is even more striking is the fact that as the son rests upon the arm of the father's easy chair the bodies of both are blended as their tailored suits appear to melt into one another. The overall impression is that the father and the son are one.

If you can appreciate what it was that Mary Cassatt was trying to convey in this portrait of the one-ness of a father and son, you have an inkling of what it was that the prophet was trying to convey in the description of godly life which he gives us in the First Reading for today. The prophet's intention was to convince his readers that God had given expression of the divine revelation of God's love and trustworthiness to the people. The history of God's relationship to the people was expressed in a history of salvation that is a tribute to God's patience and divine ingenuity. The prophet acknowledges this as having been obvious from the very beginning of God's relationship with Israel as a parent with a child reflecting the image of the parent.

**How It Is Done**

Asking people to reflect the image of God sounds like a tall order. And it would be if God did not give us the resources for doing so. However, God does give us the assurance that we can rely on God. "Blessed are those who trust in the Lord, whose trust is in the Lord," writes the prophet. Left to our own resources and relying on ourselves will always make us come up short. Tom De Haven penned a novel about the cartoonists in the era of the Great Depression. Titled *Derby Dugan's Depression Funnies,* the story relates how the cartoonists worked to ease the pain of the public during the Depression. The mythical team of Geebus and Brady produced the character of Derby Dugan. Brady produces a magic wallet for Derby that could produce a ten spot whenever needed. The public loved it.

Then there was Abe Ongo, the immortal street barber who severed hair clippings from the heads of Samson, Solomon, Julius

Caesar, Abe Lincoln, and the heads of other famous people of the past 2,000 years. Dubious at first, Geebus was inspired by the Ongo character, whose name meant he "would go on and on." It dawned on Geebus that all it would take is "one." "One guy that doesn't croak," he explained, can inspire optimism. The Depression funnies faded as America became more affluent. Yet they remain as historic reminders how people have to create their own fantasies, dreams, and mythical heroes in order to cope with the pain and hardship that come their way. The prophet would remind us that we do not have to place our hope and trust in such ephemeral characters as the characters of funny papers or any other medium. The help God offers is for real.

**The Faded Blooms**

To explain the contrast between those who rely on the Lord and those who do not, the prophet resorts to the comparison of the non-trusters with the fate of the shrub in the desert. For them there just is no real relief. We all recognize the contrast between the verdant growth when there is plenty of rain and mild temperatures to produce wholesome vegetation and those drought periods when the summer heat parches all the earth. However, the prophet makes the contrast between the growth in desert places that has no chance compared to the growth at the side of the waters that is untouched by the arid seasons. Rodney Stark, a professor of sociology at the University of Washington, published a study called *The Rise of Christianity*. The subtitle suggests that the Jesus movement became a dominant religious force within a few centuries. With the canons or rules of sociology, Stark analyzed why the pagan population decreased in the same period. In addition to epidemics and plagues, the Greco-Roman culture diminished itself by its affluence, its views on marriage, and its birth control methods. At the same time Stark ventures to say, as few sociologists are inclined to do, that the Christian believers were able to cope with problems and disasters by virtue of their faith.

The belief system of the Christian adherents was vastly superior to anything the pagan religions and cults offered through the multitude of gods they had fashioned in their idolatrous practices.

The Prophet Jeremiah claimed the same for the Hebrew faith in his day. He envisioned that the people who did not trust in the God who had been revealed in the covenant of grace were those people who were like the shrub in the desert that has to wither and fade away when the heat of troubles come. It is most certainly true to say that the Christian faith today must compete against philosophies, cults, and idolatries like those that were prevalent in the day of the prophet. It is equally true that the faith we espouse along with the prophet is superior in every way to the folly of the cultic and idolatrous practices of our day.

**According To One's Ways**

The prophet maintains that not only are the ways of the faithful superior to those who do not believe, but that God also deals with people according to their ways. That is not always apparent to us at the moment. At times it would appear that those who seize power in the world are the one's having their way. Every day we read about the struggles for power in the worlds of politics and finance. For the most part, the daily news is about the people who are successful or who fail in dealing with power. Paul Erdman wrote an exciting novel about struggles in the world of finance called *The Setup*. The story is about Charles Black, former chairman of the U.S. Federal Reserve. Charles had met regularly with nine other men representing the banking institutions of their nations. The ten men met each month in Basel to determine the fate of interest rates for the banking institutions of the world. The system depended upon the integrity and faithfulness of the players. However, Charles becomes the victim of a plot by one of the members who seizes the opportunity to make Charles the fall guy for actions that served the greed of the plotter. Eventually the plot is exposed. The story is meant to illustrate the truism that power can and does corrupt. Yet eventually, on their own terms, those who flirt with and maneuver power to their own advantage will pay the price. As the prophet says it, the Lord "will give to all according to their ways." Sooner or later the perpetrators of evil will pay a price for living according to their ways.

**Bearing Fruit**

On the other hand, it is equally true that God rewards those who draw strength and nourishment from what God offers in love and grace. As the tree that is planted by the water is able to "stay green ... and does not cease to bear fruit," the faithful are able to give and yield blessings through the exercise of their faith. The blessing for the children of God who thrive on the love of God which has been revealed to them in our Lord Jesus Christ is that they know that their lives are secure because they are able to draw strength from him who is the Living Water. Jeremiah could fall back on the tradition of how God provided water for the children of Israel when they wandered in the wilderness. As he faced the threatened future of his people who were to face the humiliation of deportation as a people into an alien nation, he could still be confident of how God would be the source of strength in the time of their direst needs. That is made all the more sure for us.

We have the history of salvation as it was lived out in the people of Israel, and they were delivered. Jeremiah's confidence that there would always be a remnant who would rely upon God as the source of their strength speaks to us, also. That becomes all the more clear as the history of our salvation comes to its climax in the life, death, and resurrection of our Lord Jesus Christ. For him the tree planted by water became the tree of the cross. So it was that the Evangelist John reports that when they pierced Christ's side, blood and water flowed from him. Obviously, it is the evangelist's attempt to help us understand that Jesus truly became the Living Water for us through all that he achieved by his life, death, and resurrection. Tragically, those who fail to trust God are the people who keep seeing oases in the deserts and wildernesses of life. There are all kinds of attractive ideas, notions, proposals, gospels, and cure-alls that are ever so alluring. However, they all turn out to be mirages, and they wither away and no lasting relief comes. For us the opposite is true. The cross is no attractive scene. However, it does reveal the truth. Our sin and our death had to be dealt with. And our Lord accomplished that for us. Our Lord Jesus Christ achieved for us the final victory over death as the true source of life. The life we live in him is the life that does "not cease to bear fruit."

*Epiphany 7*

# The Fruit Of Forgiveness

*Genesis 45:3-11, 15*

**One of the** outstanding personages of the modern era was Howard Hughes. Mr. Hughes was regularly featured in the news from the 1920s through the 1970s. He set world speed records in his day for air travel. He designed and produced new planes. He contributed much to the advancement of commercial air travel. He produced motion pictures in Hollywood and made considerable innovations in that industry. He managed and enhanced the oil drill tool industry he inherited from his father and became the second richest man in the country. All the while he built his fortune, he paid handsomely to keep his life secretive, because he believed people who are renowned should keep their lives as mysterious as possible. However, his personal life was a disaster. He courted and wooed countless Hollywood stars and starlets. He surrounded himself with a huge staff of aides. Yet all who knew him or met him consistently reported that he appeared to be a lonely man. His obsessive compulsive disorder patterns made him excessively fearful of contamination by germs, increasingly reclusive, and addicted to drugs originally prescribed for his recovery from accidents.

Toward the end of his life, an aide, George Francom, remarked to Hughes what an incredible life he had led. Hughes responded that if Francom had been able to trade places with him, he was sure Francom would be willing to swap back before the passage of the first week. Surrounded by a bevy of aides who were concerned more about what they could get from him than to care for him, Hughes literally starved to death in Mexico, forlorn and naked. Consequently, the many states in which he had operated businesses had to carry on a serious investigation into all his affairs in order to make distribution of his great wealth. When that was done, Peter Harry Browne and Pat Boeske were able to write a definitive biography of Hughes. Their account of this tortured life stands in rich contrast to the life of the handsome, rich young man Joseph, who in the First Reading for today models the fruit of forgiveness.

## The Story

Most everyone knows the story of Joseph from their Bible history lessons in Sunday school. We can use bits and pieces of Joseph's bio as they match up with the Holy Gospel for today. Joseph, like Howard Hughes, did become known as one of the wisest and richest men of his day. Joseph, you may recall, was the firstborn son of Jacob by his beloved wife Rachel. Ten other sons had been born to Jacob by his wife Leah and his wives' maidservants. Joseph and Benjamin were born to Rachel and did enjoy special favor. Joseph, like Howard Hughes, was born with a silver spoon in his mouth. Joseph was especially favored by his wealthy sheik father, because he was the firstborn by Rachel, who was Jacob's first love and favorite wife. Jacob did nothing to hide his preference for his son Joseph and blatantly displayed his favor by giving Joseph the famous coat of many colors. Joseph may have been unaware that this special treatment was odious to his brothers. Or it could be that he paraded his father's partiality for him with some abandon. The brothers accused Joseph of the latter attitude. They especially felt that way after Joseph foolishly related to them dreams in which he pictured them as paying homage to himself. That was even too much for Jacob, the father. Jacob did not think it was a bright idea for Joseph to share this kind of stuff with him and Joseph's brothers. He remonstrated with Joseph about that. At the same time, Jacob did keep the matter in his mind. The brothers could not forget the matter either.

## The Rough Years

Joseph paid a price for the favored position he enjoyed in his father's household. On one occasion Jacob sent Joseph to visit his brothers to see how they were doing as they were grazing their herds. On the spot, the brothers hatched a plot to kill the young man, but thought better of it. They ended up selling him into slavery to some Ishmalites who carried him off to Egypt. In Egypt Joseph was sold to Potiphar, a steward of the Pharaoh. Joseph gained high favor in that household and rose to a trusted position. However, Potiphar's wife also had an eye on the handsome, bright young man and enticed him to become intimate with her. Joseph's story loses all similarity with Howard Hughes at this point. Young Joseph spurns the allurements of Mrs. Potiphar. Angered by the rejection from the handsome youth, she frames him with an accusation of his harassment of her. Potiphar has no choice but to send Joseph to prison.

Joseph does not languish in prison but busies himself in such a way as to gain the status of a trustee who tends to the needs of fellow prisoners. One has to remember that Joseph had been completely on his own during these years. The parental influence is not there. His brothers had despised him and had sent him not only into slavery but also to an alien culture. There was no support system of any kind for him. There was no chaplain to visit and comfort him. There was no teacher to come and advise him. No one sent him a Bible or some devotional literature to consult or study. All that Joseph had to fall back on was the tradition and spiritual guidance his parents had shared with him. What they had shared with Joseph enabled him to remain strong and confident in the face of hardship, temptation, and trial.

**A Turning Point**

As he made his assigned rounds in the prison on one occasion Joseph noted that two of his prisoners were especially downcast. One had been Pharaoh's cupbearer and the other his baker. Both had dreams which Joseph interpreted for them. The one was favorable for the cupbearer, who returned to his master's service. The other was fateful for the baker. Two years later Pharaoh had the famous dreams which his counselors and wise men could not interpret. Then the cupbearer remembered Joseph, who was sent for to interpret Pharaoh's dreams. Joseph was set free when he successfully interpreted the dreams for Pharaoh. The dreams foretold seven years of bounteous harvests followed by seven years of drought and famine. Joseph went on to suggest a drastic program of a government-managed economy. Joseph suggested that the government create a bureau of agriculture with overseers to buy up a good portion of the produce over the seven good years and store it for distribution during the seven bad years.

Pharaoh considered Joseph's proposal a stroke of genius. He named him his prime minister on the spot. He was to be regarded as second in command over the whole land. He was bestowed with the Pharaoh's signet ring and all the accouterments worthy only of a royal family. Pharaoh gave the young thirty-year-old prime minister an Egyptian name as a sign of his adoption into the royal household. In addition Pharaoh gave his daughter's hand in marriage to the bright young man, who now had all of Egypt at his feet. Apart from the life of our Lord Jesus Christ, the story of the rise of Joseph is unmatched in all of the Scripture. Normally, all the heroic figures in the history of Israel or companions of our Lord Jesus have feet of clay or stumble somewhere along the line. Not so Joseph. We may fault him for some strange behavior with his brothers in his early years. However, he is a marvelous example of rectitude as his integrity, faithfulness, and prudence moved him along from the role of trustee in prison to a seat of power and honor in high government.

**Turnabout**

If the story of Joseph at this point were to stand alone, it would be a precious story in itself. Joseph exemplifies the kind of life that demonstrates that honesty, integrity, and faithfulness do have their own rewards. In addition, the story can be comforting for God-fearing parents about the early training of their children in the tradition of their faith. They can feel confident that the love and trust level they have maintained with their children will be invaluable when the children are removed from the home for schooling or vocation. However, the story of Joseph does not end with his rise to power. The inevitable happens. The seven good years pass. Famine comes to plague Joseph's homeland, and his father feels compelled to send his sons to Egypt to buy grain from the Egyptian rulers. Joseph recognizes his brothers, but they fail to recognize their brother who is now approaching his forties. Joseph cleverly uses the occasion to force the brothers to return with their brother Benjamin, and ultimately he reveals himself to his brothers. It is this moment of reconciliation that is played out in the Reading for today.

Joseph had instructed his servants to place his silver cup in the grain sacks of Benjamin, and then he had the brothers arrested for the crime of stealing his cup. When Joseph confronted the brothers with this staged theft, Judah stepped forward to make a plea on behalf of his youngest brother as well as for the life of his father, who would die if a second son were lost to him. Judah offers himself to be enslaved in order to have Benjamin set free. At this point Joseph can no longer contain himself. He clears the court in order to be left alone with his brothers.

**Reconciliation**

Left alone, Joseph breaks into loud weeping and identifies himself as their brother and immediately asks about his father's welfare. The brothers are so startled at his presence, they are silent. Then Joseph draws them closer to himself and identifies himself once more as their brother and adds that he is the one they sold into slavery. He does not add to his identity to make them feel guilty but rather to assure them that he is truly their brother. They have the right one now in front of them. It was like showing his credentials in order to verify his relationship to them. However, he is quick to add that they should not berate themselves or be distressed by what has taken place. The manner in which Joseph had arrived to this high station in life was God's way of getting Joseph into position so that he could be of value in saving the lives of thousands of people. Joseph mentions three times that it was God who had his hand in this. God had sent him ahead to save the lives of people, to be a father to Pharaoh. Not least, of all, God had sent him also to be able to save the lives of his brothers as well as his father. They are to return home to bring their father as well as all their families into the land of Egypt to enjoy the privileges which Joseph would be able to extend to them. With all of that, he embraced all of his brothers in tears and kissed them. This was truly the kiss of peace.

The liturgical kiss of peace which we practice in our worship services is intended to have the same effect as it did that day in the court of Pharaoh. It is meant to be the expression of forgiveness and grace between Christians. On some days it should have special significance between members of the family who that very morning had found their relationship in jeopardy. The kiss of peace in the liturgical service was never intended to be an interlude, a greeting, or a welcome between worshipers. It was meant to be the occasion for speaking the peace of God as forgiveness and reconciliation between sinners, who understand the power and the effect of God's gracious acceptance of us as a means of accepting one another.

**More Than A Kiss**

However, this excellent story about Joseph and his brothers is retold to tell us much more than just about the kiss of peace or reconciliation. The account covers some fourteen chapters of the book of Genesis. That is almost a fourth of the book. Obviously, its major intent is to show how the people of Israel develop as a people in the land of Egypt. However, it is also a classic demonstration of how God works in the lives of people. Later on, at the death of their father, Joseph once more assures his brothers of his love for them and his forgiveness. He tells them in tears as they beg his forgiveness, "Even though you intended to do harm to me, God intended it for good." By his own faith Joseph simplifies the matter. One should not get the impression that God can magically turn the evil into good. God had to do it through Joseph.

In modesty Joseph does not say that he was the one who turned it all around for Pharaoh, for the population, for his father, and for his brothers. Yet it was through Joseph that God accomplished so much. God has to put up with, contend with, and deal with the disobedience, mischief, sin, and violence that people perpetrate on themselves, one another, and the society. However, the means by which God can get to people is through people who know God's grace and love. God's people are the ones who can bring love, forbearance, kindness, and love to the world. They are the people who have to forgive much in order to win and capture the hearts of others.

**The Story Goes On**

The story of Joseph should have a happy ending. It does. When Jacob died, Joseph fulfilled Jacob's wish to be buried in the family plot of his grandfather Abraham. Joseph attended to his embalmment in Egyptian style and arranged for a funeral procession back to Canaan in regal style. Joseph and his brothers and their families returned to Egypt to live in peace and prosperity. However, the next story begins with the note that a king arose who did not know Joseph. Eventually the family of Jacob was to be enslaved in Egypt for over four hundred years. Yet once more the God of History did not forget this people and the covenant he made with their forebears. God prepared them to be a people in whom God could say all the nations of the earth would be blessed. As God had saved the family of Jacob through Joseph, so God intended to save the nations through the people Israel.

In Christ we see how God accomplished the same goals of a history of salvation through the life, death, and resurrection of our Lord Jesus Christ. God works among people to make history in the same way. God relies upon the faithful as God worked through Joseph and through Jesus to effect change by reconciliation. Theologians traditionally have not regarded Joseph as a type of Christ, because the Scriptures themselves do not name him as such. The Scriptures do name others like Moses and David as types of the Christ. However, the Joseph story is a precious gift to us in helping us to see the manner in which God is dependent upon faithful people to achieve the divine purposes and goals for the world. Joseph's story is concluded with his death at the age of 110 years, an age regarded by antiquities as befitting a faithful ruler. Before his demise, Joseph assumed the role of a prophet in speaking to his brothers. He said, "I am about to die; but God will surely come to you, and bring you up out of this land to the land he swore to Abraham, to Isaac, and to Jacob." He also left word that when his people left Egypt they should carry his bones with them, a request they fulfilled 400 years later in the Exodus. He had served his God and his people well.

*Epiphany 8*

# The Fruit Of The Word

*Isaiah 55:10-13*

---

**Andrew Goldfinger,** a physicist working with the Space Department at the applied physics laboratory at John Hopkin's University, has explored a theological understanding of creation. His work is titled *Thinking about Creation: Eternal Torah and Modern Physics*. The book is a fascinating study of how the scientific theories of the origin of the creation and the maintenance of the creation gravitate more and more to compatibility with the description of the theological understanding of the universe in Genesis 1. Currently the two scientific theories about the creation are incompatible. The theory of relativity and the theory of quantum mechanics are at odds with one another. Scientists are on the verge of creating four theories about the universe. However, as Stephen Hawkings has pointed out, science cannot be comfortable until we have one theory of force in the universe. Consequently, physicists are working hard on a theory they call "the theory of everything," TOE. This theory would unite all forces, or theories, of the universe into one. That force is hidden so deeply in everything, we consequently think there is more than one force.

However, Goldfinger points out that by faith we know that the mover and shaker in the universe is God. God, we know is so hidden in the universe that we cannot know God fully or comprehend God's person completely by our observation. What we are able to perceive is what God would have us know about God's person so that we might be in relationship with God by faith and also know what we might expect from the hand of God's goodness. The First

Reading appointed for today helps us to understand how God is the Mover and Shaker in the universe to be our Benefactor.

**The Context**

The First Reading is from one of the great poetic sections of Second Isaiah. Second Isaiah was the prophet who ministered to the Hebrews in exile in Babylonia. As First Isaiah ministered to the people of Israel before they went into exile, he called his people to repentance and faith in the light of the covenant. Tragically, he also had to foretell the doom that was to fall on them. However, he could also assure the people that God would keep the covenant God had made with them. As the people languished in the exile for decades, the Second Isaiah built on the work and promises of the First Isaiah. He called the people back to the covenant God had made. If there were those who had made accommodations to their exile and saw no future other than to prepare for a permanent stay in the land of Nebuchadnezzar, Isaiah would want them to think differently. If there were some who enjoyed the prosperity that had come to them in the sophisticated environs of Babylon, Isaiah would want to shake them loose from their complacency. If there were those who had drowned their faith in sorrow, thinking that God had completely abandoned God's people, the prophet would call them back to the faith in the faithfulness of God. If there were still others who had relinquished all thoughts about God, the prophet would revive their dead faith into a living hope.

All those whom the prophet addressed would be asking for evidences to which they could point that the words of the prophet could ring true. The way things were going in Babylon, there was no hint or inkling that the captivity in which these people found themselves could be lifted. There were no political signs on the horizon they knew of that could guarantee their freedom. While some of the captives had risen to prominence even within the court of the king, there were no indications that the exiles could muster the strength for any kind of revolt or civil action that would gain their freedom for them.

## The Creation Is God's

In typical prophetic fashion, Isaiah assures his hearers that God is not without witness. To be sure, there is much about God that is hidden from us. The prophet would not encourage anyone to tangle with those matters that we cannot know about God. Luther would add that to try to draw near to the hidden mysteries of God, we would invite nothing but disaster and judgment, for those would be the areas which God has reserved as divine prerogatives and privileges. In the section immediately preceding this reading, the prophet had written about the divine thoughts and ways of God being much higher than the earth or the thoughts of people. However, the prophet had also said that his audience should seek the Lord, because God can be found. God is not lost. God is near. God is near for all those who want to call upon him.

Mark William Worthing, a professor of Lutheran Seminary in Adelaide, Australia, has given an account of how physicists and scientists view possible scenarios for the future of the creation. His book, *God, Creation and Contemporary Physics*, cites some of the likely dialogues between theology and the physical sciences. However, much depends upon whether one subscribes to an open or a closed view of the universe. In view of the fact of an expanding universe, the universe could continue for billions of years. However, given the second law of thermodynamics, one would have to conclude that the universe is bound to die. A closed view of the universe would suggest that the universe could die from heat death in a large dark hole from which nothing could escape. Those are observations we can make from a scientific point of view. However, the prophet would have us look at much more simple evidence of the presence of God in the creation.

## The Creation Serves God

We do not have to know the sophisticated scientific theories of the nature or origin of the universe to recognize the obvious in the creation. The prophet writes that God says, "The rain and the snow come down from heaven, and do not return there until they have watered the earth, making it bring forth and sprout, giving seed to the sower and bread to the eater." God has built this natural rhythm of production of fruit into the creation for our daily benefit. We do not question that. We take advantage of the blessings that come from the hand of God. The scientists give serious study to how all of the creation works for our benefit in the effort for us to be good stewards of the creation. What the prophet would have us understand is that we should recognize that God performs the remarkable feat of providing for our tables daily. In the creation account we are told that this process of ordering the universe for our benefit began with the words from God.

Goldfinger, the physicist mentioned earlier, notes that God made ten utterances that proceeded from the mind of God to form the creation. Luther explained that we do not have to think of these as oral or verbal expressions, but rather as expressions of the mind of God. In Hebrew the words could also be thought of as "acts" of God. Goldfinger would emphasize the words expressed God's consciousness, awareness, and working of the physical universe. The word then, is the means by which God orders, shapes, and maintains life. The Hebrew helps us to understand that the word of God is not merely the word upon the page. The word of God is always the lively, active power of God exerting and expressing what is in the mind of God. The Hebrew helps us understand that best. The "word" can also be translated as "he says," or "he acts." In the word God is acting on the creation, in the creation, or through the creation. In the word God also acts on us, for us, or through us. That is the point that the prophet Isaiah wants to make clear for us.

**The Word Serves God**

Isaiah writes that the word which God addresses to us is as effective as the word by which God created and the word by which God sustains the universe. God says, "So shall my word be that goes out from my mouth; it shall not return to me empty, but it shall accomplish that which I purpose, and succeed in the thing for which I sent it." The prophet's purpose in sharing this word was that the exiles needed to know that God had not lost control of history, or more particularly, their lives, when they were taken into captivity. Contrary to all appearances, God was very much on top of things. Babylon had served God's purposes in taking Israel into captivity. It was not as though God wanted Israel to suffer so. Israel had provoked those consequences as a result of their indifference to God's word and warnings through the prophets. Now that the captives had served their time in captivity, it was time to awaken to the promises God had made them. Now they could recognize that the First Isaiah had been perfectly honest with them as he had delivered to their fathers the warnings of the inevitability of the exile. They could learn not simply from their history but from the word that interpreted their history.

Now the exiles could listen to the Second Isaiah, who came in the power and strength of God's word again. They could trust that their history and their future were assured and guaranteed by the promises of God. It is true that ordinarily the nations do not learn from their history. They do make the same mistakes over and over again. However, the people of God can learn about history from the word of God so that they do not have to be slaves to their own mistakes. They can rise above them. The people of God do not have to plunge into or be dragged into the future as victims of the moment. They can move into the future with confidence with the presence and help of God. God's word works in the world.

**No Empty Word**

The prophet witnessed to the fact that God's word was active in history. God moves history for all people. All the people of the earth are affected by the word of God's judgment. God is constantly pressing upon all peoples to make God's will and purposes work out in the world. That is true whether they recognize it or not. Nebuchadnezzar and the Babylonians were serving the will of God by taking Israel into captivity. The Israelites should have recognized what was happening, but they did not until they had sat in Babylon for seventy years. They had time to figure it out. But it was the prophet who came to figure it out for them on the basis of God's covenant. That is what the prophet means when he writes that God says, "So shall my word be that goes out from my mouth; it shall not return to me empty." In other words, the word of God is not be thought of as only some words on the pages of a beautifully printed Bible.

The word of God is actually God's power and force at work in the world demanding, pushing, and shoving people. The word of God makes people sweat as they go about their daily tasks trying to put bread on the table, striving for peace and contentment in a world where people elbow and compete with one another in trying to achieve the same goals. In that whole process God is moving and judging, rewarding and punishing. God may be judging or rewarding people. It all depends upon how the people themselves view their roles in the world. But you can be sure of this: when all is said and done, when it is all shaken down, God's purpose and will is truly done. God's word does not return to God empty. God is never just blowing in the wind. You can be certain of that. The word is God's power in action. The word is God's power working on people. That word working on people can be their salvation or it can be their judgment. But it is never without results. It never returns to God empty.

**The Positive Result**
What the Prophet Isaiah wanted the people to know is that they could look for the word to bring about positive results in their lives. No matter how remotely possible the people may have thought the possibility of being delivered from their captivity, they were to think differently. Concentrating upon the promises God had made concerning the effectiveness of God's word or promise, they could have a different feel for their future. The prophet says, "You shall go out in joy, and be led back in peace." To emphasize the possibility the prophet says that the creation which has to respond to God's word and care would cooperate. "The mountains and the hills before you shall burst into song, and all the trees of the field shall clap their hands." The reversal of the fortunes of Israel would be dramatized by the way the creation would behave. "Instead of the thorn shall come up the cypress; instead of the brier shall come up the myrtle."

Leo Tolstoy talked about how dramatically his life had changed when he came to believe in Christ's teaching. Tolstoy did not overcome his criticisms of the church. However, he does describe how his thinking was changed. What he had longed for before, he no longer wanted. What had seemed good to him before now appeared to be evil and vice versa. What was on his right before was now on his left. And what was on his left was now on his right. The prophet wanted the exiles to sense that same kind of change in looking at their situation. Instead of living by all the threats of the power structure around them, they could visualize the power as weakness that would soon falter. They could look to the word from God as to where the power and the control really were concentrated.

## A Memorial

The prophet was convinced that the day of deliverance would come inevitably. As the creation responded to the word of God in saluting the deliverance of the people, it would serve as a memorial to God. The restoration of God's people out of the exile would be one more mighty act of God. It would compare with the deliverance of Israel from its captivity in Egypt. The Exodus had been fashioned as the people witnessed how the creation cooperated and let the people cross over the Red Sea on dry ground. Now the new Exodus would be accompanied by the pleasant cooperation of creative forces that would make the wilderness seem like a beautiful garden. The differences the people would see and feel would be testimony to the presence of God.

We witness the differences in our own lives and the lives of others who have been touched by the deliverance God has effected for us by the life, death, and resurrection of our Lord Jesus Christ. We view ourselves, the creation, and everything about us in a different light. We read history that is being made in a different way than people who can see and read only how the forces of the world are at work. As the prophet dubbed the promised return of the people from exile as a memorial to God, by the gift of faith and the Spirit of God we are able to see the works of God. Luther would say that is the function of our faith. Our faith enables us to see how things really are. On the one hand, we can see how some evil and bad things are left only in the hands of people. On the other hand, by faith we are able to see God at work on our behalf. What spells the difference for us is the prophetic conviction that the word of God never returns to God empty. Our faith is not a guess as to how things will be. Our faith is not an idle hope. Our faith is based on the certainty of that word which assures us that God is at work among us. The next time you are out in the snow or the rain, remember that is God at work producing the fruit of the earth for you. Then recall that that action is parabolic of how the word of God works in the world.

*The Transfiguration Of Our Lord*
*(Last Sunday After The Epiphany)*

# Keeping The Glow On

*Exodus 34:29-35*

---

**Frank Peretti** created a stir with the publication of two books, *This Present Darkness* and *Piercing the Darkness*. He claims that his books are a creative fictional treatment about the spiritual warfare that is going on in the world. He believes that Christian people have the authority to exercise spiritual control over the things and forces which detract from the promise of what the Christian faith can be. In an interview about the nature of his books, he remarked how Christians have lost the ability to think seriously about the problems they face. He was concerned especially about the encroachment of popular culture into the life of the church. He is greatly distressed by the fact that we have raised an entire generation of what he described as "consumatons," people who have come to the conclusion that their main purpose in life is to consume things. Consumatons also believe that the most important thing in their lives is what they have just purchased.

Peretti says that this generation is so oriented to entertainment and television that if they were standing overlooking the Grand Canyon to take in the glory of the creation, they would do so for all of thirty seconds. Then they would whip around and ask if there is anything else and if the canyon does anything. What Mr. Peretti has to say rings true with many current conversations or observations about lifestyles now in vogue. Certainly it would be true that if people like the consumatons Peretti describes were to have been at the Mount of the Transfiguration of our Lord, they would have missed the glory of that occasion. In contrast to consumatons, in the First Reading for today we hear of people who wanted to keep the glow of a revelation of God's glory as Peter did at our Lord's transfiguration.

## The Parallel Experiences

One can readily understand why the First Reading today was chosen as a companion for the account of our Lord's transfiguration. In the Holy Gospel, Moses and Elijah appear with our Lord in his moment of glory. Elijah is there because by tradition he was an expected messianic figure since he had been assumed into heaven in a blaze of glory. Moses was there because tradition had it that the messianic figure would be a Second Moses or *Moses Redivivus*, Moses Revived, because his grave had never been found. Also Moses experienced a transfigured appearance when he met with God in the mount. Like Jesus, the two companions who come to comfort Jesus and talk to him about his impending death and resurrection were experienced servants of God. Moses and Elijah had been through the fires of tribulation and trial, but they had also been touched by God's glory. No one else would have been better prepared or equipped to offer encouragement to Jesus as Jesus readied himself for the ordeal of going to Jerusalem to die.

All three persons, Moses, Elijah, and Jesus, had their meetings with God in mountaintops. In the First Reading we hear how Moses met with God in the mountain. Elijah met with God in the mountain where he heard the still small voice of God to assure him that God was still present in Elijah's life and ministry. These special, unique, and revelatory experiences were intended to give comfort, approval, and meaning to ministries designed to witness to the presence of God in the lives of God's people. These revelations were never intended to be spectacular and sensational moments of when and how God comes only in glory. We shall see from the First Reading that the purpose is quite different from that. To be sure, it is good that the purpose was different. Otherwise, we should never be able to handle all the glory that is involved. We shall learn from the experience of Moses and his people that it is not easy to handle God's glory.

## The Context

The incident recited in the First Reading for today was not the first time that Moses had gone up into Mount Sinai. As it is recorded for us here, Moses had been in the mountain other times. He had received the revelation of the covenant God made with the people with the giving of the commandments. All that was revealed was preceded with the introduction, "I am the Lord your God who brought you out of Egypt, out of the house of slavery." The agreement that followed was based on the fact that God had made his claim upon Israel. God had established them as God's people by this act of delivery, this act of redemption and healing. What followed was based on the assumption that God would do for them what only a god could do for people. Then followed not only the giving of the Ten Commandments, but also the ordering of the lives of the people through social, ritual, and liturgical regulations that covered their living together as a unique people of God.

When Moses failed to return from the mountain, the people lost patience and they committed their infamous folly of making a golden calf fashioned like the idols they had seen in Egypt. Moses came down from the mountain and rectified that situation by destroying the two tablets of stone in which he received the covenant. He also destroyed the idol of the people. In hot anger Moses literally made the people digest the idol by drinking the pulverized gold spread upon water. Once more Moses went up into the mountain and received the word from God inscribed upon two new tablets of stone. On this occasion, Moses had remained in the mountain forty days and forty nights during which time he neither ate bread nor drank water.

## The New Situation

When Moses came down from Mount Sinai after this session with God, the situation was completely different. The people were most receptive when they saw Moses with the two tablets of stone on which the covenant was inscribed. The people recognized that Moses had been involved in a revelation for their benefit, and they were ready to listen. However, Moses did not sense that, because he had been in the presence of God, the skin of his face was radiant and shining. This created a problem. The people were afraid to come near Moses. That is rather interesting. Normally, people cannot get enough of the spectacular. We especially like shining things. We are attracted to the glitter and shine that make things so rich and valuable. However, this was in a man's face, the face of a man who had been in the presence of God. The distraction that caused for the people may have been simply that it was hard to listen to the man when he was shining at them like a bright headlight.

It is difficult for us to visualize this scene for ourselves. However, the inference of the record here is that the people were also afraid, because as sinners they were as much ashamed to be in the presence of this man who had been with God, as if they had appeared before God themselves. For sinners to be in the presence of God is highly intimidating. That is not God's fault. Nor does God want it to be that way. The problem is that we feel exposed for being the sinners that we are in the presence of the Holy One. That phenomenon has existed since the time when God had to hunt for the fallen creatures in the Garden of Eden, who were hiding in the bush, because they had failed to trust God. We all know the feeling. We do not even have to have done something wrong, and we feel flustered in the presence of someone who overawes us with a shining presence. We do not develop inferiority complexes. We recognize that we are inferior. In the case of the people confronting the shining countenance of Moses, the people sensed their spiritual inadequacy and their sin.

**The Remedy**

Moses did not allow the people to welch out on their responsibility to hear what had been revealed to him from God because they were so spiritually shy. Instead, at first Moses had a conference with his brother Aaron, the priest, and the leaders of the congregation. We do not know what the gist of that conversation was, but Moses must have questioned them about their reticence and asked them just how difficult it was for them to be in his presence. They must have concluded that the situation was manageable, and it was very important for the people to hear what Moses had to communicate to them. At any rate, when they broke up their conference, they gathered the people together for a session in which Moses revealed what had been given to him by God. The people adjusted to the situation and heard Moses out. When Moses finished this session, he donned a veil to carry on his normal duties and his contacts with the people.

From then on, whenever Moses went in to confer with God, he removed the veil. When he returned to the people to share once more what he had received from God, the people could see the phenomenon of the shining face. After that Moses would put the veil on again. The ritual was preserved. Undoubtedly, the routine must have been strengthening for Moses as an assurance for carrying on his prophetic office. It also must have been comforting for the people to know what Moses shared with them had divine authenticity. What began as a frightening experience for the people became a welcome ritual.

**Paul's Version**

Sooner or later the ritual had to end. The Apostle Paul writes of that issue in what we now know as the Second Letter to the Corinthians. In that letter, Paul writes a considerable amount about the nature and authority of ministry. He had been forced to defend his ministry in the congregation at Corinth, because some had challenged his right to exercise any authority over them. Paul made the argument that the members of the congregation themselves were living proofs of the validity of his work. Then he employed the experience of Moses and the people at Mount Sinai as a paradigm of the more enduring experience of the revelation God had furnished in our Lord Jesus Christ. Paul counted it remarkable that the giving of the covenant at Mount Sinai along with the law was clothed in such glory. He said if that revelation which included the law, a ministry of condemnation, abounded in glory, how much more would the revelation which God has made of love and life in the Person of the Lord Jesus be a ministration of glory.

For Paul, the revelation in Christ surpassed the former glory at Mount Sinai. Paul noted that Moses kept wearing the veil, because he knew that glory was going to fade away and die, and Moses did not want the people to see the end of that glory. So it was that later the veil in the temple was to be a symbol for the people of that glory that had been revealed at Mount Sinai, and that the presence of God was assured, but the glory remained behind the veil. So the wearing of the covering on the heads was also to be a reminder of that fact, according to Paul. For Paul, it was significant that the veil over Moses' face, the veil in the temple, and the veil on the heads of people were also symbols that the greater glory was yet to come in the Person of our Lord Jesus Christ (2 Corinthians 3:7-14). Paul was that forceful and energetic figure who had been so immersed in the Hebrew tradition as a well trained and effective rabbi. By his own experience in moving on through the radical spiritual conversion on the Damascus Road and his careful study of the life of Christ in the light of the Hebrew Scriptures, Paul understood that the glory revealed in the Person of the Christ was the greater glory. Yet for its moment the revelation of glory at Mount Sinai was glory indeed.

**Hold On To It**

One can appreciate how precious the revelation of glory at Mount Sinai was for Moses and the people. It was that way for Peter, James, and John in the Mount of the Transfiguration. Peter wanted to memorialize the moment by making a shrine. That is normal for people to create memorials to moments of glory. We do that as a community, as a state, and as a nation. We fix certain moments in our history as being essential to understanding ourselves, what we are, and how we got here. Families have ways of recalling the important events in their lives. The marking of anniversaries of more than just birthdays can be very important in helping families to stress achievements and special acts of love and service.

However, what is more akin to the revelation at Mount Sinai is what we may experience as a spiritual moment in our own lives. People can talk about a range of activities or happenings that have occurred in their lives to give them inspiration, incentive, courage, or help. That does not always happen within the rituals of baptism, confirmation, or marriage. Those provide their memorable effects. Yet the deeper sense of the divine may happen out of the blue. It may come through a song, a special word, a striking moment. It could be the experience of a sunset, a cloud formation, or some other vision within nature that provided the moment to contemplate God's glory. Whatever personal reflection one has is usually something a person wants to cling to, refer to, or dramatize in some way. It is a matter of trying to keep the glow on.

**The Best Glow**

What the Apostle Paul had to say to the Corinthians about the transfiguration of Moses was to recognize it as the ministry of glory that it was. Now, however, he says that God has removed the veil for us. We do not have to be afraid or intimidated by the revelation of glory. It is the spirit of God who has removed the veil and given us the freedom to look and to act. The veil has been removed from our faces, and by grace we have been privileged to recognize the glory of the Lord. Paul adds that not only are we able to see the glory of the Lord revealed in the life, death, and resurrection of our Lord, but also we know God's glory. We recognize the glory. However, we see the glory as though looking in a mirror, so that the glory of God is reflected in our faces, in us. The point Paul makes is that we do not have to look for the glory of God as though it were hidden, strange, and miraculous. We should know that we can see the glory of God in the face of your Christian neighbor, because we know the glory of God revealed in Christ Jesus.

Paul writes that as God said, "Let light shine out of darkness," God "has shone in our hearts to give the light of the knowledge of the glory of God in the face of Jesus Christ" (2 Corinthians 4:6). Paul is saying that what God has done for us is to permit the glory that was so evident both at Sinai and the mount of our Lord's transfiguration to be present in our lives. We keep the glow on right within our own lives as we live in the assurance of God's presence in our lives. It is by faith we know the love of God has been confirmed for us in the revelation to the ancient people Israel and in our Lord Jesus Christ. So it is that we pray in that matchless prayer of the Church on this day, "O God, in the transfiguration of your Son you confirmed the mysteries of the faith by the witness of Moses and Elijah. Make us with the King heirs of your glory, and bring us to enjoy its fullness, through Jesus Christ our Lord."

### Books In This Cycle C Series

### GOSPEL SET

*Praying For A Whole New World*
Sermons For Advent/Christmas/Epiphany
William G. Carter

*Living Vertically*
Sermons For Lent/Easter
John N. Brittain

*Changing A Paradigm — Or Two*
Sermons For Sundays After Pentecost (First Third)
Glenn E. Ludwig

*Topsy-Turvy: Living In The Biblical World*
Sermons For Sundays After Pentecost (Middle Third)
Thomas A. Renquist

*Ten Hits, One Run, Nine Errors*
Sermons For Sundays After Pentecost (Last Third)
John E. Berger

### FIRST LESSON SET

*The Presence In The Promise*
Sermons For Advent/Christmas/Epiphany
Harry N. Huxhold

*Deformed, Disfigured, And Despised*
Sermons For Lent/Easter
Carlyle Fielding Stewart III

*Two Kings And Three Prophets For Less Than A Quarter*
Sermons For Sundays After Pentecost (First Third)
Robert Leslie Holmes

*What If What They Say Is True?*
Sermons For Sundays After Pentecost (Middle Third)
John W. Wurster

*A Word That Sets Free*
Sermons For Sundays After Pentecost (Last Third)
Mark Ellingsen

## SECOND LESSON SET
*You Have Mail From God!*
Sermons For Advent/Christmas/Epiphany
Harold C. Warlick, Jr.

*Hope For The Weary Heart*
Sermons For Lent/Easter
Henry F. Woodruff

*A Hope That Does Not Disappoint*
Sermons For Sundays After Pentecost (First Third)
Billy D. Strayhorn

*Big Lessons From Little-Known Letters*
Sermons For Sundays After Pentecost (Middle Third)
Kirk W. Webster

*Don't Forget This!*
Robert R. Kopp
Sermons For Sundays After Pentecost (Last Third)